MARK RICHARDS
A Surfing Legend

Gotcha
clothes for your trip

MARK RICHARDS
A Surfing Legend

DAVID KNOX

To,
Steve "Vince" Colletta;
Keep Surfing &
Having Fun!

Mark Richards
'92

Angus&Robertson
An imprint of HarperCollins*Publishers*

AN ANGUS & ROBERTSON BOOK
An imprint of HarperCollinsPublishers

First published in Australia in 1992 by
CollinsAngus&Robertson Publishers Pty Limited (ACN 009 913 517)
A division of HarperCollins Publishers (Australia) Pty Limited
25–31 Ryde Road, Pymble NSW 2073, Australia

HarperCollinsPublishers (New Zealand) Limited
31 View Road, Glenfield, Auckland 10, New Zealand

HarperCollinsPublishers Limited
77-85 Fulham Palace Road, London W6 8JB, United Kingdom

National Library of Australia
Cataloguing-in-Publication data:

Knox, David, 1951 – .
Mark Richards: a surfing legend.

Includes index.
ISBN 0 027 174 89 X.

1. Richards, Mark, 1957 – . 2. Surfers —Australia —Biography. I. Title.

797.320994

Cover photograph by Bernie Baker
Printed in Australia by Griffin Press

5 4 3 2 1
96 95 94 93 92

CONTENTS

To Jane and Emily and to the memory of Dick Knox and Greg Studdert, true surfers. (David Knox)

This book is dedicated to the memory of my father Ray and my son Beau. If there are waves in heaven I hope that Dad and Beau are sharing a few. My father and my mother Val didn't just give me the opportunity to pursue a surfing life but taught me values and gave me strengths that have served me well in good times and bad times. Thank you Kyle and Grace, for making life so beautiful. And thank you, Jenny, for your love, your wisdom and for being there always. (Mark Richards)

Writing this book was helped by: the work of Anne Rogers and Al Hunt; encouragement from Bernie Baker and Mark Warren; the patience of Val Richards, Kyle Richards and Mick Adam; the hospitality of Jenny Richards; and guidance from Neil Jameson and Sally Harper. Inspiration came solely from the deeds and humanity of Mark Richards. (David Knox)

Special thanks to master shapers Geoff McCoy, Dick Brewer, Reno Abellira, Ben Aipa, Pat Rawson, Tom Parrish, Jim Richardson, Spider Murphy and Gerry Lopez for sharing their great knowledge and talents with me. (Mark Richards)

Photographs used for chapter openers in this book are supplied courtesy of News Limited and *Surfing World*.

FOREWORD

Australia has produced surfing champions with a frequency that astounds even the casual observer. Part of the reason for this phenomenon can be discovered in this book, which provides a first-hand account of one of the great Australian sporting champions of the post-war era — Mark Richards.

It is a commonplace observation that for every Nat Young, Tom Carroll or Damien Hardman that has graced the dais of world surfing championships there are thousands of others who surf with similar skill. Some choose not to enter the race, preferring an unsullied relationship with Mother Earth's water sculptures. Others, whether by accident or design, are not able to compete with sufficient will to win: one or two good days in the water when it's 6ft and off-shore at your home break, is one thing; to consistently surf at the peak of your abilities no matter what the conditions is another thing altogether. Champions are both born and made, as the Mark Richards story shows.

For many, surfing is the ultimate release from the pressures and pains of daily living. Champions like Richards, who managed to compete at the very highest levels, often under considerable pressure, generate a kind of aura and mystique. To surf well requires a creative individual response to situations that range from the mundane to the terrifying. Victory, whilst offering the opportunity for some financial security, can often be a mixed blessing. There are many talented surfers who have OD'd on a little fame and fortune but it comes as no surprise that Mark Richards kept his head through the help of supportive parents and a clear sense of belonging that came from a lifetime of surfing Newcastle's beaches.

I first met Mark Richards when he came to compete in a SAND (Surfers Against Nuclear Destruction) competition at Duranbah sponsored by Midnight Oil in the mid-80s. Whilst Mark was not known for taking a strong stand on issues such as competing in South Africa, as some of his colleagues did, I found his presence at contests of this kind, where there were no flash prizes or big cheques, very encouraging.

On that day as always, his surfing was stunning. An extraordinary coexistence of grace and aggression on the wall of the wave. Like all champions he made what was incredibly difficult seem easy. But most impressive to me was the fact that the champion was a person who did not put himself above other people. He had managed to maintain his sense of balance and empathy with the community of everyday surfers and situations. That in itself is as singular an achievement as the number of trophies he collected whilst dominating world surfing for years.

Surfers of all ages are only too aware that our precious coastline is under incredible pressures. To preserve and protect the headlands, estuaries and beach breaks from development and pollution will require every single person who has enjoyed the sea to be prepared to give up time and energy for her protection. It is a reassuring thought that great champions are prepared to speak out and to act so that we all might continue to surf clean water.

Mark Richards has experienced the highs and the lows. He has tasted the rare joy of complete mastery of his chosen skill. In his family life he has suffered tragic loss. Through all of that, he has remained a quintessential Australian: down to earth, with a strong sense of affinity to his home, and not given to hyperbole or self-promotion. Good on you mate. I hope everyone enjoys your story as much as I did.

PETER GARRETT
JULY 1992

PROLOGUE

A surfer paddles into the wave and eyes its smooth, beckoning face. As he gets to his feet on his board he keeps a close watch on how the contours of the wave are shaping. He drops to the bottom and sees the wall steepen sharply. He can make a long, drawn out turn that will safely ensure he outruns the threatening curl or he can drive his board hard and vertically to the top of the wave where, with a violent contortion of his whole body, he will snap the board round in the tightest of arcs, falling with the lip and setting himself up for another turn at the bottom of the wave.

Contest surfers, like divers, gymnasts or ice dancers, can determine the degree of difficulty with which they perform manoeuvres on a wave. Unlike the other sportspeople, they cannot notify the judges beforehand because their medium — the waves — constantly change. Judges of modern professional surfing contests will award points for the most radical manoeuvres performed with control in the most critical part of the wave. Surfers who try the difficult moves in more challenging situations take the greatest risk, but if they succeed, they will beat surfers who take a more conservative approach.

The margin between degrees of difficulty can be infinitesimal. In the 1985 final of the BHP Steel International at Newcastle, the veteran Shaun Tomson of South Africa, and the emerging Tom Curren of California appeared evenly balanced as they produced exciting state-of-the-art surfing. But a closer look revealed that Curren's turns from bottom to top were a few degrees closer to vertical than those of Tomson. Those few degrees were enough to give Curren the decision.

As with motor cycling and formula one drivers' championships, the professional surfing world championship is decided by the accumulation of points awarded for results in contests that make up the world circuit. For example, a contest winner may earn 1000 championship points to the runner-up's 860 and the third placed contestant's 730 points. Mark Richards reigned supreme for so long because more than anybody else he could meet the judging criteria in the greatest range of waves. He accumulated more world championship points than any other surfer from 1979 until 1982 by riding the best waves for the longest distance, and performing the hardest and most radical manoeuvres in the most critical parts of the waves.

INTRODUCTION

Mark Richards thought he was about to drown. He was at Waimea Bay, a picturesque cove on the north shore of the main Hawaiian island of Oahu. It was 7 December 1986.

He watched a giant wave fold neatly before him about 20 metres away. 'This is it,' he thought. 'I'm going to die.' The circumstances of his impending demise didn't surprise him. After all, he had been surfing for more than twenty years and was on his sixteenth trip to Hawaii. The irony that he would drown in the Billabong contest in front of peers, friends, admirers and anonymous spectators struck him momentarily. But the overriding emotion was the fear, the bowel-loosening terror that goes with confronting huge waves at Waimea Bay. To be caught in such a situation where the ocean has taken over and you have lost control of your destiny, haunts every surfer with its inevitability.

Most days of the year Waimea Bay is a tranquil, sandy inlet with a beach that is less than 100 metres wide. A Catholic church overlooks the bay, which is at the end of a lush, green valley, home of the beautiful Waimea Falls. As the northern winter swells get bigger, Waimea Bay loses its attraction to the casual swimmer. Waves begin to dump very heavily on the shore while further out, waves begin to fringe the rocks on the northern side and slam into the menacing outcrop on the southern side.

Adventurous body boarders and body surfers come to tackle the pounding shorebreak and surfers ride the fat, relatively unexciting waves next to the northern point. When the swells reach a certain size, the shorebreak becomes far too dangerous to ride and the main break shifts out to a submerged rock plateau off the northern point. Huge swells travel unimpeded for thousands of kilometres before hitting this submarine shelf, where they steepen dramatically and break ferociously.

The middle of Waimea Bay is so deep that it is rare for a wave to break right across it. On this day, however, the swell was so big, not even the depth of the canyon next to the impact zone could prevent the bigger waves from breaking.

Mark Richards saw a set coming and 'when a set comes at Waimea the horizon goes dark. In Australia you just see a bump out to sea, but at Waimea the whole ocean goes dark at the horizon and you are confronted with this colossus of water. It's like getting a Manhattan-sized skyscraper, dropping it on its side, painting it black and sending it charging toward the beach.' He saw the caddies (surfers with spare boards for competitors) paddling frantically and 'then I realised the set was so big it was going to close out the Bay. The first wave reared up and it was probably about 25ft and I was paddling like there was no tomorrow, as were the others behind me, and then the wave broke right in front of me, top to bottom, 20 or 30 yards away, this giant wall of white water . . . I was so mesmerised and so terrified by the wave I didn't really dive. I just slid off the side of my board. I got rumbled around but the worst part was being dragged along by my board. I was wearing a 12ft and a 6ft leg rope tied together and it was like skiing underwater. I thought my leg was going to get ripped off.'

Miraculously, Mark Richards finally got to the surface and reeled his board in. Eighteen feet of leg rope had been stretched to almost twice its length. 'From that moment I felt I was invincible at Waimea because nothing worse could happen.' He became selective, choosing only the bigger waves which he surfed with stylish expertise in what was tantamount to an exhibition heat in giant Waimea.

In that heat and the next, which he also won, the judges awarded Mark perfect 10 scores for two of his waves. Randy Rarick, one of the north shore's most experienced surfers and observers, believes that Mark rode a 25ft wave that day — a feat very seldom accomplished even in that arena. James Jones, one of the great big-wave riders in Hawaiian history, isn't renowned for his quickness to praise. But when Jones, twice winner of the Duke Kahanamoku Classic, bumped into Mark a few days later he said, 'That ride was incredible'. Jack Shipley, Hawaii's most experienced contest judge, said that if the Eddie Aikau Memorial big-wave event, open only to invited big-surf specialists, had been held at Waimea on 7 December 1986, Mark Richards would have won. Shipley said it was arguably the best Waimea had been ever ridden.

'Forget the finals. Just stop the contest and give it to the guy' was the succinct observation of a spectator. He summed up the feelings of many who had witnessed the world's finest surfer enjoying one of his finest hours.

CHAPTER ONE

NEWCASTLE:
HEAVEN ON EARTH

A survey in 1991 found that people who live in Newcastle, Australia's sixth biggest city, regard it as the closest thing to heaven on earth. This finding was greeted with much derision for the industrial city on the New South Wales coast, 160km by road north of Sydney, has seldom been regarded in a celestial light. A visitor's abiding memory is a grim skyline of vast furnaces and belching chimneys. Australia's biggest public company, Broken Hill Proprietary (BHP), has a huge iron and steel works operation alongside Newcastle Harbour.

The port, which is at the mouth of the Hunter River, is also a major loading dock for the coal that is still mined extensively in the region. It was this coal that prompted the British to establish at the beginning of the 1800s the first mainland penal colony outside what is now Sydney. Convicts were sent up from the original Australian settlement to mine the coal in the most primitive, foul conditions. They also

Richards displays his inimitable grace as he prepares to turn off the bottom at Pipeline, Hawaii.
PHOTO: JEFF DIVINE

Off the Wall, Hawaii 1975. During this visit to Hawaii Richards moved towards riding his own equipment. PHOTO: PETER CRAWFORD

Off the Wall, Hawaii 1976. Here he shows the same classic style as in the 1990 shot used on the cover of this book. PHOTO: BERNIE BAKER-LEONARD BRADY/ISLAND STYLE

Mark's parents, Val and Ray Richards.

gathered the lime from the vast oyster beds and defoliated the coastline as they harvested huge reserves of cedar. For more than 20 years Newcastle was a gaol, a hell-hole closed to all except the labouring convicts and their guards. From these harsh, inhuman beginnings developed a prosperous town whose surroundings were rich in natural beauty and valuable resources.

In the austere 1950s Newcastle, its lifeblood very much BHP and the mines, was a quiet, uncomplicated place where the work ethic reigned supreme and free, imaginative thinking was scarce. Newcastle was a safe, comfortable city with no major crime problem. As with the rest of Australia, sport played a big part in people's lives and Newcastle was legendary as the breeding ground for great football players.

Newcastle accountant Ray Richards had not been able to play football. A hip complaint had stopped this active,

'I still enjoy being around Mum': Mark with mother Val.

energetic man from doing anything that involved running. So Ray and his wife Val developed a passion for the water. In the summer they looked forward to the weekends when they could get away from their jobs at the Wire Rope Works and head for the beach. The sun and the surf were their great loves.

Like many young men Ray Richards wanted to get on in the world and he knew he had more chance of doing that by working for himself. Australia had begun to shake off its post-war rigours and as more wealth was distributed the demand for motor cars began to increase. As the price of a new vehicle was prohibitive for most, Ray Richards saw his chance to become a second-hand car dealer. With the help of a bank loan he established a showroom at the far western end of the city's main commercial thoroughfare, Hunter St, which ran for 3km from the 'top of town'.

Ray circa 1960, already pointing out the ways of the ocean to young Mark.

Crouched and driving: surf-o-plane rider Mark Richards at Kirra Beach, Queensland, around 1960.

Never far from water: Mark, aged three, in Queensland.

When you're only three years old, a 4ft 6in surf-o-plane seems enormous.

Right: At three years of age, Mark already had the poise of a true surfer.

Below: Mark, almost five years old, with sun protection.

Val and Mark Richards at Blacksmiths Beach, just south of Newcastle, around 1960.

This is easy!': Mark, aged two, showed early promise.

The Richards' second-hand car and surfboard shop in Newcastle, around 1959. The cars eventually gave way to surfboards.

The venture worked and Ray and Val Richards began to make a living from selling cars. They set up house in an apartment above the showroom to which they brought home their only child, Mark, who was born at the Mater Misericordiae Hospital in the western suburb of Waratah on 7 March 1957.

From the outset Mark joined his parents on their cherished trips to the beach. Though he loved to swim in the ocean, Ray Richards never joined the surf lifesaving clubs that were so much a part of Australian beach culture before the explosion of the surf craft industry.

In the late 1950s Ray Richards saw somebody riding waves in Newcastle on a malibu board of the type that was becoming popular after the 1956 visit of some Californian lifeguards, including the great Greg Noll. A few enthusiasts in Sydney had begun shaping and glassing the balsa boards so Ray Richards, keen to tackle this new sport, travelled down to buy one from Barry Bennett, a pioneer of the industry who was still running a flourishing business in Brookvale more than 30 years later.

The only other craft being ridden in Australia in those days were short, rubber surf mats or the huge, cumbersome, plywood paddle boards and skis used by the surf lifesavers in their races. The malibu, as has been well documented, revolutionised surfing. As Ray Richards became more proficient on his new toy, beachgoers kept asking him where he got it. They were amazed by the manoeuvrability of the short boards and intrigued by the possibilities of what could be done on them. So Ray Richards made another telling business decision. He returned to Sydney and bought several boards from fledgling manufacturers, such as Bennett and Gordon Woods, and put them in his showroom alongside the second-hand cars, so establishing what has become one of

Mark's second board, a
Woods 'wafer', at
Blacksmiths Beach in
1966.

Australia's oldest surf shops. Sometime in the early 1960s, Ray Richards sold his last car and went into the surf business full time.

For a surf-struck youngster that shop was a wondrous place. Magnificent, shiny, multi-stringered surfboards festooned the walls and gleamed on their racks around the room. High on the walls were huge posters of surfers riding ridiculously big waves at unheard-of places in Hawaii.

Out the back there were even more boards and in the pokey little office Ray Richards had jammed all the paraphernalia of surfing, including exotic, glossy magazines from California that sold for seven shillings and sixpence (75 cents) and had pictures of surf stars doing amazing things on seemingly perfect, glassy waves.

This was the environment in which Mark Richards was

His first surfboard: at the age of six, Mark was dwarfed by his specially made Gordon Woods, shown here with the Blacksmiths breakwater in the background.

nurtured. Ray and Val worked long hours at the shop but they still found time for their trips to the beach. They put an inflatable rubber ring on Mark when he was a toddler and taught him to swim in the saltwater baths just a few hundred metres from Merewether Beach. Young Mark was put on an incentive program. The harder he worked at his swimming, the closer the Robin Hood and William Tell fan got to a new bow and arrow set or, a little later, a new surf mat. Ray was a Catholic, though non-practising, and so he and Val sent Mark to the nearby Sacred Heart Primary School run by the Sisters of Mercy. In those days if you went to a Catholic school in Newcastle it was fairly certain that you would wind up playing rugby league football. Mark was bigger than the other boys and so often was the first one picked for the teams: 'I don't have fond memories of being in football teams. Nobody ever told you where to stand and I had no comprehension of where I was supposed to be on the field so I never really enjoyed footy. They just assumed you would know the field positions.'

But summer was a different story. There were the trips down to Blacksmiths Beach, about 15 minutes drive south of Newcastle. Like the suburb of the same name, Blacksmiths is flat, stark and starved of greenery but as the beach is sheltered from most swells by a long breakwater on the northern side of the entrance to Lake Macquarie, it's an ideal beach for beginners.

A couple of Mark's friends from Sacred Heart, Steven O'Connor and Greg Corrigan, would often join the Richards family on their days out at Blacksmiths. They were Mark's cricketing pals and basically, they surfed because he did. Mark worked his way up to a 4ft 6in surf mat, which was long enough to stand up on as he rode the small waves at Blacksmiths Beach. He had already become a proficient

Mark with his first Midget Farrelly board.

swimmer and could handle himself well in the protected waves at Blacksmiths and the long, gentle swells of Queensland's Rainbow Bay, where the family went for their annual vacations.

To be riding a surf-o-plane, as the inflated mats were called, at such a tender age was prodigious, though Mark had no idea he was doing anything exceptional. He got his first board when he was just five years old, which was about six years before most kids graduated from the soft surf-o-planes to the hard, heavy boards that by this stage were built mainly from polyurethane foam, rather than balsa.

At about the same time Australian Midget Farrelly was beginning to have an impact on the international surf scene, Mark Richards was taking his first, unconvincing steps toward greatness on his first surfboard. 'It was a red Gordon Woods with white GT stripes on either side. It was 6ft long [about 3ft shorter than most boards of the day] and had been made from the front of one blank and the end of another because they didn't want to waste a whole blank on such a little board. I was so excited I thought this is going to be the ultimate. Finally, I've got a surfboard. But the trouble was I couldn't get into waves on it. The first day I rode it the wind was howling offshore at Blacksmiths and the waves were very small and full and I would paddle on to the wave and just get stuck at the top. I was a bit disappointed. It wasn't as great as I thought it was going to be because I didn't get many waves.'

Still, Mark, who must have been just about the youngest surfboard rider in Australia, persisted. Ray had taken him to surf movies and they had left a vivid, if not particularly positive, impression: 'I watched people in the movies surfing Waimea and Pipeline and getting murdered and I thought they were lunatics. The manoeuvres they were doing, the size of the waves, were way beyond my comprehension. There was no way I would want to do that and even if I was stupid enough to do it, I never would be brave enough to tackle such waves. It's still pretty stupid when you think about it.' Mark doesn't remember purposefully trying to improve his surfing, 'though I suppose I must have. Surfing was not nearly as manoeuvre-orientated in those days. You would catch a wave, stand up, make that first turn and ride across the wave. Today when kids go surfing regardless of age or experience they want to try to do all the advanced manoeuvres such as aerials before they have even learnt the basics. They want to do the things they have seen in movies and magazines. But back then there were hardly any manoeuvres. You just concentrated on trying to catch a few waves and ride them from the outside to the beach without falling off. It was a very relaxing form of surfing, not like now.'[*]

For the six years or so after he was given his first surfboard Mark continued to surf at Blacksmiths at the weekend and in Queensland on his holidays. His only claim to fame in those pre-teen days was the fact he was the son of Ray Richards, by now a mogul in Newcastle surfing. This was the 1960s and surfing in Newcastle, as in most seaside communities, had boomed. A young surfer called Lloyd 'Sam' Egan had gone on from fixing the dings in his friends' surfboards to setting up his own custom surfboard business — Newcastle's first. Clubs were being formed, talented young surfers were building reputations and in 1965 the city staged Australia's first 'professional' contest, an event held in conjunction with Newcastle's annual Mattara festival. Surf stars from up and down the east coast of Australia hit town in the quest for the cash and product prizes on offer. There was

[*] Mark's recall of those earlier, mellow days are ironic. He later became probably the most gymnastic of surfers as he advocated his 'rip, slash and tear' approach to riding waves.

even a Californian, Bill Wetzel, in the contest but his visit was marred by a marijuana bust, another sign of changing times within surfing.

Mark's other great passion was cricket. 'I loved cricket. I probably played as much cricket as I surfed in the early days. I had my own bat and ball and there was nothing I liked better than staying after school and playing cricket. My friends would come over to the house and we would play in a lane behind the surf shop. I was obsessed with cricket, much more so than with surfing. I could do it, my friends could do it whereas surfing was just something you did on the weekends.'

Unlike so many youngsters in Newcastle, Mark lived a few kilometres from the beach so, at least until he was in his mid-teens, he was unable to join in the pre-school and after-school surfs and swims that were a regimen for the luckier kids who lived in beachside suburbs such as Stockton, Bar Beach and Merewether. Even later he had to rely on his parents for transport to the beach, as Val recalls: 'We had a few fights when it was time to come home. It would be getting pitch black and I would be thinking we'll never get any dinner tonight and I would switch the headlights on. That was the signal to get out of the water but by that stage the lifesavers' flags would not have been down for very long so it was an open go all over the beach. He would be a surly little monster when he came in under those circumstances.'

But while the weekends at the beach were fun, surfing was by no means occupying Mark's mind day and night. There was an unusual aspect to Mark's boyhood. The surf shop was in a business and light industrial area, well away from the suburban neighbourhoods of neat homes on quarter-acre blocks separated by grey paling fences. Because of his inaccessibility, young Mark had few friends and didn't grow up exposed to the beach's youth tribal cultural with its mores

Casual matador: Richards comes face to face with a magnificent wave at Haleiwa, Hawaii, in 1976.
PHOTO: BERNIE BAKER-LEONARD BRADY/ISLAND STYLE

Direction change: Richards puts his back to the test in 1976.
PHOTO: BERNIE BAKER-LEONARD BRADY/ISLAND STYLE

Richards in Hawaii in the mid 1970s, a time when he was just starting to consider surfing as a viable career. PHOTO: PETER CRAWFORD

and pecking order. 'I couldn't just drop into someone's place and they couldn't come over to mine anytime they liked. I mean, I had no next door neighbours or in fact any neighbours.'

Despite the odd situation, Mark has no memory of an unhappy childhood. His closest friends seem to have been his parents, a closeness that continually endured and strengthened. Many years later he told an interviewer he had always been a loner, particularly when he was travelling the world circuit. 'I enjoy staying by myself and doing what I want to do when I want to do it. I've never really been a group traveller'.

In 1967, the year after Nat Young won the world title in San Diego, California, surfing underwent an enormous upheaval. Australian surfboard shaper Bob McTavish had signalled the changes in 1966 when he began to develop slightly shorter, thinner, lighter surfboards of the sort Young rode so powerfully and aggressively to victory in San Diego. McTavish, an excellent surfer and a robust, intelligent individual, had put a lot of thought into surfing, boards and waves. He was a free-thinking experimenter who was constantly looking at ways of getting more out of surfing. McTavish wasn't satisfied with simply perfecting the time-honoured, graceful Californian style of surfing. Aided and abetted by another extremely original thinker, Californian kneeboard rider and maker George Greenough, McTavish began to explore ways of putting a surfer into situations on a wave that had never before been attempted. For a laboratory McTavish, Greenough and Young used the long, peeling point breaks of New South Wales' north coast and Queensland's Gold and Sunshine Coasts. They began to fiddle with bottom, fin and rail designs and in 1967 they took the major step of taking several feet off the length of the surfboard. They reasoned the only way to become truly involved in the most critical part of a breaking wave was to have equipment short enough to fit in there. Greenough already had the answer with his flexible kneeboards and surf mats, but McTavish and Young wanted to expand the possibilities for stand-up riders.

There was some resistance to their radical new boards but eventually Australians and then the rest of the world embraced the new technology. On one memorable day late in 1967 at Honolua Bay on the Hawaiian island of Maui, Young and McTavish demonstrated with their fantastic surfing just how much more scope the short, manoeuvreable boards gave a surfer.

The first short boards were primitive by today's standards, but the move away from the traditional malibu board was one of the most significant eras in surfing's brief history. This epic period swirled way above young Mark Richards' head, but he was about to make his own great leap forward, thanks to a broad-smiling, laconic surfing champion called Robbie Wood.

Out of the water for once: Mark in his early teens.

CHAPTER TWO

REBEL
WITH A CAUSE

The civic leaders have cleaned up the Merewether Beach foreshores but it's still a fairly barren, stark place. Merewether is the southern end of a 2km long strip of sand not far from Newcastle's central business district. At the northern end is Bar Beach, a haunt of retired captains of industry and commerce and society women from the nearby wealthy suburbs of Bar Beach, The Hill and Hamilton South. In the 1960s it was home to some of Newcastle's better surfers such as Ross Ferris and Bob Lynch, but it never established itself as a seat of power in the surfing world. Because Bar Beach has always had tables, chairs and showers it has remained a meeting place for ever-changing groups of regulars. Just down the strand are The Cliff and Dixon Park, which haven't had a readily definable local crew since the very early 1960s. Both these sections of the beach offer superb waves in the right conditions.

Next along is Pogonoski's, named after a prominent family of local commerce who had their home just above this strip of beach. Mark Richards and his family now live in a timber and glass, two-storey home overlooking the beach. The Richards' house has been designed to offer clear views of the southern extreme of this strip of beach, which is called Merewether, after the adjacent suburb. There's the usual sand beach and further to the south is a rocky outcrop off which there are several reefs that can provide some of the best waves in Newcastle.

Merewether has played an important role in the development of modern surfing in Newcastle with its influence apparently strengthening rather than diminishing. But before anyone ever rode a surfboard at Merewether there was the surf lifesaving club, which has produced national champions and has played host to major carnivals, including the Australian championships. Merewether may not be the prettiest beach but it's a place of waves, an energetic arena that attracts surfers anxious to test their skills.

In the late 1950s Merewether was an old coal mining community, which was rapidly becoming another bastion of middle-class Australia because of its twin attractions of the beach and proximity to the city. The local youngsters had leisure time on their hands and some of their families could afford to buy them surf-o-planes and the new malibu surfboards that were becoming so popular. A surfboard was a precious item in those days and they were built to last. The early Merewether surfers began tackling the excellent waves that broke outside the unforgiving rocks. Unlike just about every other major surfing spot in Newcastle, if you lost your board at Merewether there was almost always a price to pay in shattered fibreglass and gouged-out foam.

In 1959 one of Australia's first surfboard clubs was formed at Merewether; Robbie Wood was a founding member. A skinny larrikin who had formed a deep and abiding love of the ocean, Robbie was very much an outdoor kid of the rough and tumble 1950s. He played football, he fought, he skipped school, he scorned authority, he had a penchant for mischief and he drove too fast. Yet for all his wildness, Robbie was a leader. He organised his friends into forming a club when it looked as though the beach authorities might make life unbearable for them. The first club faltered, but in 1964 it was reformed and Robbie was a driving force in its organisation and its fund-raising.

There was an aura about Robbie. Most surfers liked him. His sheer bravado and his smooth style in the biggest of waves commanded respect. Robbie helped Ray and Val Richards in their surf shop on busy Saturday mornings. It was a shrewd move. The chance of buying a block of wax from a surfing hero must have attracted plenty of youngsters to the Richards' shop. As Mark grew older Robbie, by this stage a married, self-employed businessman, began to take an interest in nurturing the youth's surfing talent. As Mark recalls: 'Rob was one of the best surfers in Newcastle at the time and he almost always surfed at Merewether. It had some of the most challenging waves because waves broke next to or behind the rocks and in those days, before leg ropes, only good, or foolish, surfers rode there. Robbie would work in the shop on Saturday morning and in the afternoon he would get me away from Blacksmiths by taking me to Merewether or Leggy Point.'

The latter surf break, usually referred to as Glenrock Lagoon in those days, was an excellent but remote spot just south of Merewether. Its sylvan setting belied the fact that the point was at the southern end of a beach closed to public use because it was the site of a sewage treatment works. Robbie Wood and fellow Merewether surfers Jim Newburn and Phil Woodcock were among the first to surf the powerful right handers that broke next to the rocks at Leggy Point. Like Merewether, a lost board at this place could have disastrous consequences, a fact that as Mark remembers, never deterred Robbie: 'I had always thought Rob was a bit of a looney because he always went out when it was really big. It was Rob who started dragging me out into bigger waves on those Saturday afternoons at Merewether and Leggy Point. I was scared because the surf was so much bigger and more challenging than Blacksmiths. I was very wary about going out there some days but Rob was totally gung ho. He would urge me to go out with him, saying I had nothing to worry about because he would be out there to make sure I didn't get into any trouble. I suppose I couldn't have asked for a better person to get me into big waves.'

Taking young Mark surfing seemed a natural thing to do for Wood. His friend Ray wasn't always available and Mark had no way of getting to the beach himself. And it soon became apparent to Robbie Wood that the boy had unusual talent: 'He picked it up so quickly. He obviously had above-average talent. The balance was there right from the start. He got it from riding surf-o-planes. He would come out on big days and though he wasn't doing too much, no fancy turns or anything, he was taking off. And he was only eleven years old.'

Mark's involvement in surfing was gathering momentum. In 1969 he began high school at the Marist Brothers' College in the nearby suburb of Hamilton. The old, conservative Catholic school laid heavy emphasis on discipline, academic success and sporting accomplishment, particularly rugby

Mark Richards, aged
eleven, strikes a
perfect position at
Blacksmiths Beach.

Blacksmiths Beach on Christmas Day 1967. This wide-legged stance was reminiscent of Kevin Parkinson, NSW junior champion at the time.

Already radical: Richards, aged eleven, surfs Schnapper Rocks, Queensland.

league. But Mark still didn't care much for football so sports stardom, Marist Brothers style, was to elude him. By this stage, however, the surf bug had bitten.

Thanks to his parents' ferrying duty, Mark was now surfing regularly at Merewether alongside some of Newcastle's finest surfers such as Peter Cornish, Peter Thomson, Jim McInnes and Ian Moore. It was tough just getting a wave sometimes in what could be a ruthless and crowded line-up. From the mid-1960s, Merewether had quickly built up a large band of good and highly competitive surfers and as the battle for waves became more intense, attitudes became more uncompromising. In those days Merewether typified the best and worst of surfing. Some of its 'characters' were ill-mannered and combative as they strove to get the best waves. Mark Richards stepped into this cauldron and, as he has done throughout his life, managed to find his way without making enemies.

At Wood's suggestion, Mark joined the strong Merewether Surfboard Club. His first attempt at competition, in a club contest, was a dismal failure but he soon began to establish a reputation in club, regional and state contests. Although Mark was later to become one of the sport's great champions, he was certainly not a large fish in the small pond that was Newcastle junior competition in the early 1970s. He had many proficient rivals.

Baby-faced and street-wise Peter McCabe was another youngster who embarked on a fairly undistinguished academic and football career at Hamilton Marist Brothers in 1969. Answering to the unflattering nickname of 'Grubby', McCabe shared Mark's love of surfing. He was a denizen of town beaches such as Nobbys and Newcastle and the minuscule cove between them called Cowrie Hole, the site of true quality waves.

The late Jim McCabe
and Mark Richards
before a heat of the
Newcastle
championships,
Catherine Hill Bay,
1969.

Mark Richards hangs five at Surfers Paradise, Queensland, 1968.

McCabe and his lookalike younger brother, the late Jimmy McCabe ('Little Grubby', naturally) were fantastic surfers whose talents were being encouraged by the city beaches' senior citizens, just as Mark was getting the push from Wood and the Merewether elders.

Extraordinarily, out in the south-eastern suburb of Redhead, in the neighbouring Lake Macquarie Shire, there was yet another prodigy who was soon to lock horns with his city peers. He was a laughing, affable knockabout called Colin Smith. Considering the still relatively compressed nature of Newcastle surfing it was amazing that Richards, Peter McCabe and Smith would go on to become world class surfers.[*] A fierce and highly successful competitor in his early and mid-teens, McCabe later eschewed contests as he built a

[*] Mark has reiterated over the years that the main reason Australia has produced so many successful competitive surfers is because the amateur network in Australia provides such a great training ground.

solid reputation as one of the great free surfers, particularly in the testing, hollow waves of Bali. His economical, position-conscious style owes much to his early idol, the great Hawaiian surfer Gerry Lopez.

Colin Smith was a working class boy straight out of the unprepossessing mining hamlet of Redhead. He was also an enormously gifted surfer who developed a passion for big waves. Though his professional career never quite took off Smith, the 1978 Australian champion, managed to win a contest in big surf at Sunset Beach and won the qualifying trials at Bells Beach in 1978, the same year Mark won the first of his four main events at the annual Easter contest in Victoria.[*]

From the beginning Mark had two highly talented and

[*] A heavy smoker, Smith died from lung cancer in 1986. One of his last heroic acts was to appear on a national television current affairs program to encourage youths not to smoke.

The late Colin Smith (left) with Ian Moore (centre) and Mark Richards (right): schoolboy medal winners, Manly, 1968.

keenly competitive surfers to ensure he learnt the hard way. Competing against, and sometimes losing to, McCabe and Smith was an ideal preparation for Mark and an early exercise in humility. 'My parents were acutely aware of me doing well in contests and were always anxious I didn't turn into a big head,' he recalls. His ascent was rapid but he cannot recall any one event that prompted him to think there may have been some sort of future in surfing. Competing, like surfing, was simply fun.

In the late 1960s and early 1970s Newcastle had a flourishing surfboard association with much spirited competition among clubs. For the better surfers there was a formalised, highly structured process of graduation through state and national levels to the world championships. These were held every two years, but lapsed after the 1972 titles and were resurrected as the world amateur titles in 1980. Mark won the New South Wales title in 1972 and 1973, and in big surf at Margaret River he also won the Australian junior title in 1973.

In 1972 Mark got a taste of things to come when he was chosen for the Australian team for the world titles in San Diego. The titles turned out to a fiasco, but the trip for Mark was an eye opener. 'I was too naive,' he recalls. 'In those days fifteen-year-olds weren't as sophisticated as they are now. All the other surfers in the team were older than me and it seemed like they were always off chasing girls. We had no manager and there wasn't even anyone to meet us at the airport. Ian Cairns and Mark Warren looked after me. I couldn't get out of the place quickly enough. The surf was terrible and Ocean Beach in San Diego seemed to me like the strangest place on earth. It was Californian beach culture at its most bizarre.'

During that contest Mark had the first of many tussles with the great Hawaiian surfer Michael Ho, who went on to place fifth overall. Their first encounter nearly reduced Mark to tears. 'Michael really worked me. I've never forgotten that. He always has been a ferocious competitor. He kept getting inside me and there was nothing I could do about it. I had never been in as intense a competition as that.'

On the way back from the world titles, Mark, Tony Hardwick and North Narrabeen's Col Smith stopped off in Hawaii. It was Mark's second trip to Oahu's north shore, having been there in March 1972 in what was a shoddily-arranged expedition. He rode small waves, mostly at Rocky Point, and gained a glimmer of recognition from some film coverage and an honourable mention from the great Barry Kanaiapuni in a magazine interview.

People had begun to take notice of his ability, but surfing for Mark was still just a leisure pursuit. Then in 1973, the year he won the national junior title, the sport in Australia took its first small step toward professionalism when the annual Bells Beach Easter event offered cold hard cash.

Surf-related industries were growing and offering more opportunities for people to base their lives on surfing. Midway through the year Mark Richards quit school with some vague notion he could make a living out of surfing. Though English had been his strong subject, his great love had been woodwork and he had the germ of an idea that perhaps a job shaping surfboards would help him keep body and soul together and give him the time off he needed to go surfing.

As a teenager, Mark Richards succumbed to the surfing bug and began to contemplate a career in surfing. PHOTO: SURFING WORLD

CHAPTER THREE

MAN
OF VISION

Ray Richards allowed his son Mark to leave school in the fifth year of what was supposed to be six years of high school. By this stage surfing was Mark's life, his *raison d'être*. At his father's intervention he had been taking approved time off from school to travel to contests and he had already made two trips to Hawaii that had also cut into school time. Each time he returned to classes he found it harder to make up the lost ground and his schoolwork suffered. 'I can't remember if I talked my father into letting me leave school or whether it was his idea or whether we just came to a mutual conclusion that it was time to can school.'

Though he had passed the legal school-leaving age and had acquired his School Certificate after four years of junior secondary school, the decision to drop out could have been seen as a rash move. Particularly when the reason was to concentrate on his surfing career. What career? In those days society viewed people who surfed and didn't work at conventional jobs as misfits and layabouts. The hippie movement had infiltrated deep into the surfing culture. Conventional wisdom was that many surfers were long-haired, aimless drug takers. The sport was going nowhere and neither were its devotees. While such recollection does contain a fair amount of generalisation, it would be safe to say many people would have looked askance at Ray and Val Richards for allowing, and even supporting their son in his quest of a dream. But Ray Richards was nobody's fool. Perhaps he, far more than his son, had an inkling of the future. Val Richards describes his attitude: 'Ray was a pretty liberal thinker. He did not have a straight tunnel vision and he wasn't a rigid disciplinarian. He insisted that Mark go to school and even had him tutored in maths so he would do well in his School Certificate. But half-way through fifth form he could see Mark was not applying himself to his study and he couldn't see the point in keeping him at school. Mark had no aspirations to be a doctor or whatever. In those days if you left school after fourth form you became an apprentice tradesman, that was the norm. So Ray told Mark he could leave school then and he could have a year at surfing and if he wasn't going anywhere at the end of that year he would have to get a trade or do something else positive in regard to his future. Surfing did have a hippy image. Primarily the reason people thought surfers were layabouts was because they had long hair and they were breaking out, questioning the rigid structure we all followed in our youth. It was amazing the number of parents who created scenes, telling their kids to get their hair cut. There is so much more freedom these days. Really, the hippy period gave everyone a much broader vision, an alternative to the ridiculous rigid morality that was the go in our youth, and allowed people to lead a much freer life. Ray hated the earlier rigidness so he did not insist on Mark conforming to it as he grew up. Yet he did insist he went to a Catholic school because Ray was a Catholic, though not practising. In those days if you were a Catholic your children went to a Catholic school.'

The truth about surfers in the late 1960s and early 1970s was often obscured by poor, biased unprofessional reporting and comment. People at the forefront of the sport at that time included Nat Young, Midget Farrelly, Paul Neilsen, Mark Warren, Peter Townend, Ian Cairns, Narrabeen's Colin Smith, Terry Fitzgerald and Simon Anderson. They had long hair and they did question some traditional values. But all these surfers and many like them were clever enough or lucky enough to find ways of making a living by capitalising on their talents and reputations. All are now active surfers who have succeeded in fields such as manufacturing, commerce and the media. They have families and they are respected members of their communities. They are not ordinary people, by any means, but neither are they greatly different from so many who have achieved something in their lives. Most have found ways of putting something back into the sport that rewarded them so richly, if not necessarily in a material way. Surfing did have its casualties. Its culture was more clannish, more tribal in those drug-influenced days and for some the thrill of just surfing simply wasn't enough. Some died, and some destroyed their minds and bodies with their excesses.

For many surfers these days a tidy living can be made just by being good enough to gain sponsorship from clothing companies or surfboard manufacturers. But twenty years ago for most good surfers, apart from an elite few, sponsorship meant getting your new board at cost price. So the early professionals needed ingenuity. They shaped boards, they swept up in board factories, they served in surf shops, they made wax, they wrote articles for surfing magazines and newspapers.

Seventeen-year-old Mark Richards, a skinny kid with an odd style of surfing that made people sneer, stepped straight from school into this existence. Mark's routine became daily surfs at Merewether, often with Ray's binoculars trained on him from the carpark, and then back to the shop to help his parents or to work on his surfboard-shaping skills. There was never any notion that he would just hang around the beach between surfs. No son of Ray and Val Richards was going to be a beach bum. For Mark this was never really an option: 'I've never been a beach person. Strange as it may sound I actually don't like lying around on the sand, sunbaking. I like to surf, shower and go. And I'm not a very social person so there was never the attraction of just hanging around at the beach talking to my friends.'

By this stage Mark was riding boards shaped by Geoff McCoy who had also enlisted the talents of North Narrabeen surfers such as Mark Warren, Grant Oliver, Colin Smith and Tony Hardwick. Mark smiles at the suggestion that he had tapped into a limitless supply of free boards. 'I always paid for my boards,' he says. 'I didn't want to feel obligated to anyone. That way if you didn't like somebody's boards you could just up and leave.'

Mark often surfed with highly competitive and ambitious McCoy riders, sometimes at North Narrabeen, probably the most talent-laden beach in Australia at the time. His reputation developed but in 1974, although he reached the junior finals of the Australian championships on the Gold Coast, he could manage only a fifth in defence of the title he had won at Margaret River, Western Australia, the previous year. It was off to an inauspicious start, but

1974 was to be a watershed year, not just for Mark but for
Australian surfing. For the second year running the contest
at Bells Beach was offering cash prizes and Mark was
granted entry into the invitation-only field, which included
Hawaiian visitors Jeff Hakman, Barry Kanaiapuni, Gerry
Lopez and Reno Abellira. Mark put on a respectable
showing, as he did again a month or so later in the
inaugural 2SM/Coca-Cola Surfabout in Sydney when he was
again the youngest in the field. Coca-Cola's first foray into
professional surfing is a landmark. The company's
association with the sport has endured and it has ploughed
far more money and promotion into surfing in Australia
than any other sponsor. Mark is in no doubt about the
importance of the company's role in professional surfing's
development. [*]

In 1974 Mark Richards finished seventeenth in the
Surfabout, but he was a delighted young man. He was surfing
against and sometimes even talking to the world's great
surfers, people he knew only from magazines and movies.
Now he could watch them surf close-up and talk to them
about surfing and his awakening interest in surfboard design.
It was a thin, cashless time for the youngster but it was rich
in treasured memories. 'I remember once I gave a lift to the
great BK [Barry Kanaiapuni] from Narrabeen down to Fairy

[*] When Coke announced a promotion linked to the annual Coca-Cola Surf Classic in
Sydney early in 1991 some professional surfers were outraged. Winners of a pick-the-best-
wave TV competition were to be given starts in the prestige event, regardless of surfing
ability. Even the Association of Surfing Professionals, so dependent on Coke for this and
other contests, couldn't hide their dismay at the prospect of a non-surfing couch potato
being given a prized spot in the year's second richest contest on the world tour. Mark
Richards saw things differently. 'Coke *are* professional surfing and I reckon they are entitled
to do what they like,' he told the *Sunday Telegraph.* 'It's very hard to criticise Coke because
of the tremendous support they have given surfing over the years. You have all these one-off
sponsors of tour events, but without Coke there is no such thing as professional surfing in
Australia.' After this ringing endorsement of what many still believe was an ill-conceived
and foolish stunt that grossly insulted professional surfers, the controversy evaporated.

Bower. I mean, there he was, The Man, with the killer bottom turn at Sunset, a full legend, sitting next to me in my car. All I could think of was I hope I don't have an accident and hurt him.' Kanaiapuni survived the drive and the two became firm friends. Mark wandered wide-eyed through that contest, which he describes as more of a 'happening' than the ruthless, results-are-everything events of today. 'Basically the only person I knew was Rabbit [Bartholomew] but the other surfers, most of whom were much older than me, were pretty friendly. It was a great time. It was more like an exchange of ideas, having all these people from different countries in the one place at the one time.'

Later in the year Mark, though still eligible for the juniors, entered the more lucrative open division of the Mattara event, now held at his home beach Merewether. He comprehensively won the final from surfers such as Mark Warren, Colin Smith (Narrabeen), Peter Townend, Peter McCabe and one of his early surf trip 'chauffeurs', Merewether stalwart Dennis Bridges.

His reputation grew. A few months later he returned to Hawaii on his fourth trip. Though he didn't even reach the final of a contest this was to be perhaps his most momentous stay in Hawaii, the time in which he squared up to Waimea Bay, to a career in surfing, to destiny. He was seventeen years old. He had never really contemplated going out at Waimea, but he had made it through to the quarter-finals of the Smirnoff Pro (now defunct) and was staring at some of the biggest waves ever ridden at Waimea Bay — let alone in competition. That day Mark Richards made one of the most momentous decisions of his life. He believes that if he hadn't paddled out into one of the biggest days ever ridden at Waimea Bay, his life would have followed a very different path.

The first day of competition was at Sunset Beach and when Californian Tiger Makin didn't show up for his heat, Mark Richards got the call ahead of the shattered Wayne Bartholomew and Shaun Tomson.[*] In a noble gesture, Bartholomew lent Mark the entry fee for his last-minute start. Sunset is one of the world's great surfing beaches. Huge peaks break heavily on to shallow coral anything up to a kilometre off the narrow beach. While surfers at Waimea ride simply to survive, Sunset's smaller and much longer waves offer the surfer a challenge to perform. At Sunset the rider can choose the degree of difficulty. The reward is pure excitement. The penalties include energy-sapping, hold-downs under mountainous white water, bloody maulings on the razor-sharp reef and severe injury just from the raw power of the waves.

On a board he had borrowed from his board shaper, Geoff McCoy, Mark Richards paddled out into his heat with some of surfing's greatest stars of the time, including Hawaiian Larry Bertleman. According to Mark, 'The surf wasn't that big. About 8–10ft and mellow, fairly subdued for Sunset so I charged into the middle of the peak and started taking off.'

In the process, Mark discovered within himself a quality that would be largely responsible for his ascent to surfing greatness. 'I call it coloured singlet mentality. It's something I have relied on ever since. You put that competition singlet on and logical thought gets thrown out the door. Self-preservation disappears. You just want to win the heat whereas in recreational surfing you might think "Whoa, if that wave lands on me I might drown or get hurt". I forget

[*] Mark believes he was given preference over Tomson and Bartholomew because he had written to tournament director Fred Hemmings supplying his impressive contest record and requesting a start.

about things like that when I'm competing. I just go for it. I was just amped at getting into the contest and amped at having Bertleman in my heat.'

Mark put in one of the day's more spectacular displays and won the heat. Bertleman was second. Both went on to qualify for the next day's semi-finals.

The swell leapt overnight so the contest organiser Fred Hemmings, the 1968 world champion and an autocratic figure who later pursued a career in Republican politics, moved the contest to Waimea Bay. When Mark arrived at Waimea the next day it was sunny, the wind was light offshore and the waves were huge. 'Rumours had begun the previous day that it would be at Waimea. That was for madmen and heroes. I wouldn't even dream of going out there. I really just wanted to walk back to the car and drive home and hide. This was after I had seen a 30ft set close out the Bay that morning.'

The world's finest big-wave riders such as Barry Kanaiapuni, Sam Hawk and the Aikau brothers Eddie and Clyde were insisting to Hemmings that the surf was too big for the contest. But Hemmings had other ideas. He had worked hard to establish the Hawaiian events and gain extensive television network coverage. He wanted the contest to go on. Mark Richards, the gawky youth from Australia, knew from Hemmings' demeanour that the contest would be held. 'Fred said "Hey, you guys, the TV's here, the wind's offshore, it's a beautiful sunny day. It's going to be unbelievable. This will be the biggest event in the history of surfing. It will cement the future of surfing." '

Hemmings had a vision and would not be swayed by the surfers' reluctance to risk their lives. He played his trump card in the battle of wills by offering to go out himself, an ultimatum the surfers knew he could, and would, make good.

Mark Richards stood at the crossroads. He could pull out and nobody would think any the less of him. He was, after all, only seventeen and with no Waimea Bay experience. But something gnawed at him. He felt, deep down, that to walk away would consign him to oblivion. He could forget about his dream of revolving his life around surfing. Going back to a trade apprenticeship in Newcastle held no appeal. So out he went, with basic survival uppermost in his mind.

It is difficult to explain to a non-surfer the skill, fitness and commitment required to ride big waves, particularly in Hawaii where they break with so much power. A surfer, a board, a wave. It seems so simple. Yet only a minute percentage of surfers ever achieve any sort of mastery of truly big waves. Randy Rarick has ridden some of the biggest waves ever to break on Oahu's north shore for the past 30 years and he still dreads the moment every winter when he realises he may be caught by a Waimea monster. Mark paddled out and decided to just sit on the shoulder. 'But then as soon as the siren blew I took off on a wave that just appeared right there in front of me. It was the most unbelievable feeling. I probably hadn't ridden a wave half as big as that one ever before. I remember that Waimea feeling of weightlessness as you stand up and look over the edge and that moment when you're suspended. You actually stop for a split second because there's so much water rushing back up the face. Then you reach that point where the momentum really gets you and you go shooting down the face. I became gamer as the heat went on and in the end I was actually bottom turning. I got a fourth and it's the only event I've been in where I was actually relieved when they read the names out and I hadn't reached the final. Great, I thought, I don't have to go back out there.'

Mark Richards signalled to the world that day that he would become great. More importantly, he proved to himself he could not only ride big waves but that he could do it well and that he actually enjoyed it. Mark's dilemma that day was mirrored in the 1986 Billabong contest when young Australian professionals Gary Green and Bryce Ellis withdrew from their heats, saying it was too dangerous. The implications of their decision were enormous. Here were ostensibly two of the best surfers in the world declaring publicly they weren't equal to the conditions that day. They provided fuel for professional surfing's critics, particularly the macho big-wave fanatics of Hawaii who scoff at the structured world circuit as a gaudy contradiction of what real surfing is all about. Green's lack of experience in Hawaii rendered him less than equipped for Waimca's huge waves. Later he was quoted as saying of his decision to pull out: 'It's there in the back of my mind, yeah, and it will be for the rest of my life, I think. Not meeting the challenge.' For Ellis, a strapping, health-conscious surfer from Avoca on the NSW Central Coast, the decision was simple. 'It was not a bad move. Waimea at 20ft is actually a pretty easy place to surf, but that day it was 30ft and closing out. That's when you die,' Ellis said later. 'I didn't cop any flak over that decision. Nobody hassles you for not going out when Waimea is like that.' Mark Richards is all for people being aware of their limitations but in light of his own choice and its ramifications, he remains unconvinced Green and Ellis made the right choice.

The following year Mark returned to Bells Beach for the third professional running of the annual Easter contest. He came a highly promising fifth, his surfing and contest abilities growing all the time. He earned $500, his biggest payday so far. Queenslander Michael Peterson, almost invincible in the early 1970s, made it three victories in a row at Bells under the old objective judging system in which surfers were awarded set amounts of points for each manoeuvre. As Mark recalls: 'For those few years Michael was the best. His manoeuvres were so much faster, and of course in that system they counted every wave you caught. One of his big advantages was that he was an exceptionally strong paddler. He could catch 10 waves to every one else's five. But he would have won anyway because he was a better surfer than anybody else. The speed at which the guy surfed was amazing. He was going fast when everyone else was going slow. He was coming hard off the bottom and hitting the lip. He was surfing the critical part of the wave and that was when boards were a little longer, around the 7ft mark. A lot of people were surfing out in front of the curl but Michael was always tight to the curl and he, like Rabbit Bartholomew, had an unbelievable knack of getting inside the tube.

'In those days the organisers used to publish a list showing how many points were awarded for each manoeuvre. I remember being near his car at Bells and looking in through the window. He had the list stuck to his dashboard so he could memorise it. I thought "This guy's going to win this thing again".'

Michael Peterson, a taciturn, enigmatic man, won the Australian titles in 1972 and 1974, the Bells event in 1973, 1974, and 1975, the Surfabout in 1974, the Mattara in 1975 and the inaugural Stubbies in 1977. An instinctive and brilliant competitor, he was probably the best surfer in the world for several years. Beset with personal problems, however, he then faded from the scene, particularly as professional surfing became more structured and more public and went in search of the corporate dollar. While peers such as Wayne Bartholomew, Shaun Tomson, Mark Warren, Ian Cairns and Peter Townend were consummate performers in front of a microphone or a television camera, Michael Peterson was reticent and shy.

Peterson had taken over from Nat Young as Australia's leading surfer. Where Young was extroverted and very comfortable in the public eye, Peterson was the antithesis of the polished public performer. Many years later his reticence and general behaviour drew sharp criticism from South Africa's 1977 world champion Shaun Tomson, who accused Peterson of holding professional surfing back in Australia. Tomson said it was not until Richards and Bartholomew took over from Peterson as the country's leading surfers that the sport was able to fulfil its sponsorship potential. Mark is not as caustic in his recall of Peterson's contribution but he agrees with the gist of what Tomson said: 'That is pretty right because Michael was just Michael. He was obviously ill at ease at presentations and he didn't say anything in terms of thanking the sponsors or in promoting the event. Surfers now are pretty much accepted as normal athletes but in those days the public perception of surfers was poor and I think that what Shaun was saying is that Michael's behaviour reinforced people's views about surfers.

'There is more to being a professional surfer than just going out there and riding a board. I read a story the other day that is really true. It said the pay cheques of all the young guys now contain the blood of Bartholomew, Richards, Townend, Cairns, Warren and Tomson. I don't think these guys today appreciate it. They see it as a God-given right to be paid to surf. At the last Coke contest [1988] I surfed in at Manly, I saw surfers running away from the TV people when they tried to interview them. It is not hard to stop for two seconds while a guy asks how did you go and you say good or bad.

'I guess you could say that without Shaun, Bugs, myself, PT and Ian and a lot of the people who really put a lot into it and tried to project a good image of surfing that these guys might not be making the money they are now. I really do not think they appreciate it and I don't think they realise how fragile the whole thing is, too. Surfing is not like a mainstream sport such as tennis or golf and I think they have to make some effort to publicise it and do whatever they can to put something back into it and not just take, take, take.'

The Surfabout in 1974 had generated much interest and the sponsors, Coca-Cola and the radio station 2SM, put up the money and support again in 1975 for the moveable event on Sydney's northern beaches. Events in those days had waiting periods and flexibility of venue to capture the best conditions possible. The events were packaged mainly for television unlike the one-site contests of today that sacrifice conditions to cater for spectators.

In 1975 Wayne Lynch, one of the most gifted surfers in the history of the sport, had come out of competitive retirement after winning four successive Australian junior titles from 1967 to 1970. Lynch had mystique. He came from the Victorian resort town of Lorne and first gained recognition in 1965 when, as a fourteen-year-old, he reached the semi-finals of Newcastle's Mattara contest competing against probably the most talented field of juniors ever assembled in Australia. He was extremely young, his vertical style was exciting and original and he received an extraordinary push from the surfing media, particularly surf writer John Witzig and his brother, Paul, a film maker. He went on to star in Paul Witzig's films *Evolution* and *Sea Of Joy* and after an unenthusiastic performance at the 1970 world titles in his native Victoria, pretty much disappeared from the public eye.

But in 1975 he was back and in a superb reminder of his dazzling skills Lynch won the second Surfabout from a strong field. Runner-up that year was a quiet, shy youngster from Newcastle, Mark Richards. He remembers the contest: 'Second was pretty good but I remember I was really disappointed I didn't win that one. I was in with a really good chance to win it with one round to go. It was the points-for-manoeuvres system and the scoring was relative to who you had in your heat. In the last round I was in with a group of people who weren't in contention and they were mucking around. For instance, Buzzy Kerbox was out there on a really long board and he was getting a lot of the better waves. But Wayne Lynch was in a heat that was really competitive with a few guys that were in contention. I know you should never ever say I could have won if I had heard the siren or if I had used the right wax or if I had known the heat was 30 minutes instead of twenty-five. You should never make excuses. But I feel if I had been in a more competitive heat or in a heat with Wayne I might have won. One half of me was elated at having done so well and the other was disappointed at not having won. That's how it is in contests when you come second. You're so close yet so far. The only thing that matters, the only thing that people remember, the only thing that goes into the record books is who won.'

Coming second to Mark means nothing. It's a non-achievement. 'If you reach the final and you come second it means you may as well have stayed on the beach for that 30 minutes or whatever. Wherever you come in a contest, apart from first, you will resolve to do better next time. The only person who can be really satisfied after an event is the person who wins. That's the only time I was ever completely happy. Regardless of all that crap of "You gave it your best shot, you did your best under the circumstances", you're never really happy unless you win.'

In his farewell amateur appearance, Mark Richards came second again, this time to Terry Fitzgerald in the Australian championships held for the first time in South Australia.

Mark returned to Hawaii late in 1975 on his fifth mission to the Islands. By now, especially after the year before when he had faced up to giant Waimea in the Smirnoff, Mark wasn't just a confident big-wave rider. He was hungry for big surf: 'I had become acclimatised to the fear factor. I had learned to live with it. I was on a really good program that year. The previous year I had stayed with all the Australians in a house at Rocky Point and it didn't work. With only one or two cars you invariably end up surfing places you didn't really want to surf or you stay somewhere longer or shorter than you wanted. So I figured the best thing to do was set myself up and have my own car.'

With the help of Hawaiian champion Reno Abellira, Mark organised accommodation with Audrey Sutherland right on the beach between the popular surfing spots Chunns Reef and Laniakea. Mrs Sutherland was the mother of brilliant surfer and 1966 world championship finalist Jock Sutherland, after whom Jocko's, the left-breaking reef straight out from her home, had been named. Much happier with his independence, Mark launched himself into an extensive surfing schedule as soon as he arrived in Hawaii.

His preparation paid off. After scraping through his first heat of the Smirnoff he went on to reach the final at Waimea Bay, which was in a decidedly more mellow mood than the previous gigantic year but still big and challenging. He scored an outstanding victory over Ian Cairns and Wayne Bartholomew: 'The other guys had some really bad wipeouts and I think that knocked them around a bit. I somehow managed to find a niche for myself. In those six-man heats the guy who could stay away from the hustling usually won. It was a close one between Ian Cairns and myself. The wave that won it was a really clean-faced wave. I actually did a bottom turn and went up the face of the wave and did a cutback about half-way up this 20ft wave. It exploded above me and I became engulfed in white water and I remember thinking if I come out of this I'll win. I was crouched in the full death stance and I was saying to myself "You've got to come out of this. If you can hang on you'll win." And I did.'

Mark Richards and Wayne Bartholomew had entered the water as rank outsiders against Cairns, Reno Abellira, Jeff Hakman and Shaun Tomson, all previous winners in Hawaii. Suddenly Mark was $US5000 richer and a bona fide superstar. He pulled off an unprecedented feat when a little later he won the Men's Cup, which had taken over from the old Hang Ten contest and in turn became the World Cup, still a part of the world professional tour. It was the first time a surfer had won two major events in the same season. Now he was $US9000 richer. As Mark explains, it was also the beginning of the whole Australian push in Hawaii. 'We had a completely different attitude in the way we attacked the waves. The Hawaiians were a little more laid back, a little more soulful. They tried to flow more with the wave but the thing the Australians were trying to do was to translate their small-wave surfing into their big-wave surfing. We tried to do the same things on those big open faces that we were doing on small waves while the Hawaiians were striving for speed and position.'

`Mark Richards is one of the most explosive, radical and incredible surfers I've seen,' Ian Cairns said in 1976. PHOTO: PAUL SARGEANT

The laid-back Hawaiians had nowhere near the same focus on winning as the aggressive Australians, who had been reared on a dizzying round of club, regional, state and national amateur competition. They were battle-hardened and once they mastered the Hawaiian conditions they became formidable competitors.

Mark's main memory of the Men's Cup was that he snaked Reno Abellira for a couple of waves: 'I felt really, really bad about doing it because he had made me the boards that had gone so well for me in the Smirnoff and that contest. But I couldn't help myself. I just went for the inside, the whole contest terror tactic. I felt bad about it while I was doing it but not after I got the wave. Reno Abellira was one of the few people I've known who have left me dumbstruck when I've spoken to them. He was such a fantastic surfer, had such a great sense of position. When he won the Smirnoff the previous year I was completely in awe of how he rode those huge waves at Waimea Bay. He rode them with such composure.'

But in the heat of the moment such adulation was forgotten as Mark Richards purloined Reno Abellira's waves in what turned out to be a dream contest. Everything came together for Mark in the 8–10ft glassy Sunset Beach surf and he rates that victory as one of his more emphatic. 'My surfing had a symmetry about it. My wave selection, my timing, my feet positioning were all spot on. And after I won that final I wore a grin for a week. It had been my dream to win a contest in Hawaii and now in the space of weeks I had won two. Here I was surfing with my heroes and beating them. It was unbelievable. There are times when you feel you can do no wrong. The Men's Cup, the 1975 Smirnoff final, two Gunston finals in South Africa and the first Billabong final felt like it. You feel invincible. You know the writing's on the wall and that you are going to win. '

Speaking to *Surfer* magazine at the end of the 1975–76 season, Ian Cairns said:

Mark Richards is one of the most explosive, radical and incredible surfers I've seen. And he's going to improve outrageously. He's got an untapped amount of talent. He's emotionally sound — he won't be a one-day fizzle. He'll be around for a long time. He's a tremendous surfer. And he'll be the guy to beat consistently in the future anywhere in the world. He's good in small waves. He's good in big waves. He's just a well-rounded, incredibly hot surfer. I don't go for his style. It's not relaxed or eye-pleasing, but the manoeuvres and positions he gets into on the wave are phenomenal. I reckon he's a progressively exceptional surfer.

Mark Richards returned to Australia and after a suggestion from a friend, Hawaiian cameraman Ronny Romero, he began riding a futuristic, highly manoeuvreable 6ft 8in sting design surfboard made by the great Hawaiian surfer/shaper Ben Aipa. He still has the board, which is one of his favourites. He rode the Aipa board into sixth place at Bells behind winner Hakman and then after a slow start comprehensively won the 1976 Surfabout and added another $A5000 to his swelling bank balance. 'I thought I was rich but in those days $15 000, which was about how much I had won in the past four or five months, was a lot of money.' A naturally kinetic surfer, Mark found he could turn the sting on a much tighter circle and under the points-for-manoeuvres system being used in the Surfabout for the last time his intensified frenzy made him unbeatable.

Despite becoming surfing's richest money winner, Mark

Richards was still unsure about the viability of a career simply surfing. He began to develop his interest and skill in surfboard shaping, believing it to be his real future. 'I still didn't see a big future in pro surfing or the fact that you could make a lot of money from it. I was always really conscious of that thing about "What are you going to do when you grow up?" I had to have something to fall back on.' His interest in shaping had been awakened at a very early age when he stayed with Geoff McCoy in Sydney and watched him work. 'I felt that was my calling in life because it related back to the creative side of school, the part I had enjoyed so much.'

For the rest of 1976 and in 1977 and 1978 Mark went through a transitional period as he began to experiment with surfboards and began moving towards riding his own equipment. During this time he won only one event, the first of his four Bells Beach titles in 1978, but he also made what he regards as the most important move of his surfing life. He began to develop his interest in surfboards with two fins: 'The start of the whole twin fin resurgence, which is directly related to my whole career, winning four world titles and everything, happened at the Coke contest in 1976. That's when Reno appeared with his little fish twin fin. It was only 5ft 3in and something like 20in wide and even though he wasn't doing the manoeuvres the other guys were doing he was generating phenomenal speed in small waves. I thought that maybe this was the way to go. I was beginning to have problems with single fins in small waves. Because I was around 12 and half stone, I was bogging down in small waves. It was becoming increasingly apparent that waiting periods for contests were being phased out and they were to be held on a weekend-to-weekend basis, more often than not in small waves. I felt I needed something to get me going in small waves and that's how I became interested in the twin fin and in Reno's surfing.'

Mark was still happy with the sting that he had won the event on but began riding an Abellira-designed, Richards-shaped twin fin on small days back home at Merewether. He returned to Hawaii for an extra long stint in the 1976–77 season when, at his father's suggestion, he paid expert shaper Dick Brewer to teach him the skills of shaping. Mark had definite thoughts about design but his hands couldn't do what his mind commanded so he took lessons from one of the most influential characters in surfing.

Brewer was the iconoclast who became an icon to his devotees. A judge at the Makaha championships in the 1962–63 season, Brewer is credited with defying tradition and giving extra points for Midget Farrelly's acrobatic, flamboyant, hot dogging, so helping the young Australian pull off an upset victory over the graceful but less active Hawaiians. Founder of the Surfboards Hawaii label, this pioneer big-wave rider became one of surfing's great shapers. Mark left nothing to chance in a month of comprehensive tutelage. 'Everything I do now is based on his style of shaping,' he says. Brewer made Mark a revolutionary twin fin, characteristics of which Mark combined with aspects of the Abellira twin fin to make his own twin fins. Now he had found the answer. 'They were fast and manoeuvreable. I felt like I could do anything.' He took his twin fins back to Hawaii for the momentous 1977–78 season, in which Tomson's tube riding and Mark Richards' rip, slash and tear approach ushered in a highly publicised new era.

A highly talented band including Mark Richards, Mark Warren, Shaun Tomson, Michael Tomson, Ian Cairns and Peter Townend gravitated towards a north shore spot called

A triumvirate of gentlemen. Richards with friends Shaun Tomson (left) and Mark Warren (centre), at the Coca-Cola contest held at Narrabeen Beach, NSW, in 1979. PHOTO: PAUL SARGEANT

'Off the Wall' — a short, hollow, right hander that also attracted a platoon of film makers and magazine photographers. Mark recalls that 'competition for critical acceptance as the best surfer, not just the best contest surfer, became very intense. Also, we were all out to see who could get the most photos. It was very self-centred. I would cringe if I saw Shaun getting a tube because I thought that could make a cover shot so I would try to counter with some big, off-the-top move. Mark believes the result of all this rivalry was an unofficial tie between Tomson and himself. 'Unquestionably, Shaun was the winner in the barrel and I was the winner out on the face.'

Back in Australia in 1978, Mark rode his twin fin to third place in the Stubbies, losing to Wayne Bartholomew in the semi-finals. A month later, however, he reversed the result in an epic final at Bells Beach. Mark has ridden hundreds of thousands of waves yet the wave he caught to clinch that final remains vivid in his memory. With about five minutes to go Bartholomew, in position, let an unpromising wave go and Richards, holding a slender lead, took what many thought was the wrong option by catching the wave. To this day he's not sure why he did because the sensible strategy would have been to 'sit' on his opponent and perhaps finish off the heat with a big wave: 'I dropped into it and it was perfectly smooth and it was about 5 or 6ft with a long square wall. Sometimes in competition you hold back a little, just keep a bit in reserve because you go for the percentages. You don't want to fall off. Better to get an 80 per cent finished ride than a 100 per cent face plant. But on this wave I remember I just decided to pull out the stops. I came zinging off the bottom and the top of wave formed up beautifully. It was just inviting to be hit. It wasn't too flat and it wasn't too critical so I pulled off a huge carving turn off the top and as I came out of the turn I heard Rory Russell, who was commentating, exclaim over the microphone "Whoa, MR, what an off-the-lip!" and I remember thinking as I came down to the bottom "Wait till you see the next one" and I did another one and then another one. I knew I had won after that. I walked up the beach and I was thinking "I've won a Bell". That was it, I wanted to win that trophy.'

Colin Smith, Marks' old sparring partner from the amateur days in Newcastle, won the trials final. Beaten but never bowed, Bartholomew went on to win the third world title in 1978. Mark still had no great interest in pursuing the circuit, but in 1979 that was about to change.

CHAPTER FOUR

THE
ACCIDENTAL
CHAMPION

Mark Richards' first world championship was something he neither planned nor expected. At the beginning of 1979 the man who was already being hailed as the best surfer in the world or at least the best competitive surfer had no designs on this new, still rather loose concept called the world title.

Despite its arguably non-competitive nature, surfing has always had a preoccupation with who is the best at a local beach, in the country or in the world. The sport is, after all, a contest between a surfer and the ocean. While contest surfing today is highly structured and formalised and while certain etiquette should be observed in free surfing, the actual pastime of riding waves has no rules. There are no set-out playing fields, no time constraints, no umpire. One of the peculiarities of this most selfish of sports is that a surfer needs nobody else. A body surfer doesn't even need equipment. It's just a surfer and the ocean.

Yet for all their sport's freedom, surfers have always asked and set out to determine who is the best. In the early days when Hawaii was the centre of the surfing world it was broadly accepted that Duke Kahanamoku was its greatest exponent. The Duke was one of surfing's most enduring and charismatic personalities. A Waikiki Beach boy and Olympic swimming champion, Duke introduced surfboard riding to Australia at Freshwater Beach in Sydney in 1915 and helped to popularise surfing in California.

As surfboards became shorter and lighter and the sport began to appeal to more people, surfing's hub switched to California and its glassy, usually small waves. Through the 1950s and into the 1960s, surfing expanded rapidly in California as the sport's industry and media began to develop. During this time many fine surfers were exposed to a surfing public hungry for knowledge of the burgeoning sport. Until the explosion of popularity in California in the early 1960s, there was still little by way of competition except for the annual Makaha contest in Hawaii and the Huntington Beach event in Orange County, California. The legendary George Downing won the first Makaha event in 1954 and local board maker Jack Haley won the inaugural Huntington Beach event in 1959.

The man many considered to be the greatest surfer of the period was a stylish, innovative Californian rider called Phil Edwards. Much of Edwards' reputation was built by hearsay, though the early surfing films helped to reinforce the opinion that he certainly was a leader in the sport.

Edwards was an innovative surfer in the early 1950s because he began exploring different ways of riding a wave. While most surfers were content to glide across the wave on their big, cumbersome boards, Edwards and the other hot doggers of the time experimented with manoeuvres that ultimately would accomplish what every surfer aimed for — proximity to the most critical part of the wave. An expert of style and control, Edwards also had great agility and his powerful, aggressive approach in all sorts of surf helped to lay the foundations for today's ultra-energetic, acrobatic surfing.

In the 1960s surfing contests mushroomed and in May 1964 the first world titles were held at Manly Beach, Sydney. The women's winner was Queenslander Phyllis O'Donnell and the men's winner was Sydney surfer Midget Farrelly, whose victory at Makaha 18 months earlier had been an important catalyst in surfing's huge surge of popularity in Australia. World titles, open to all comers, were held again in 1965, 1966, 1968, 1970 and 1972 and when the event was revived in 1980 in France, it was restricted to amateurs. The world amateur championships are held every two years and attract teams from many countries.

It's ironic that the 1970s gave birth to professional surfing because this was the sport's most esoteric era. Gone were the competition stripes, surf teams and razzamatazz of the early and mid-1960s. No longer was there any discussion about getting surfing into the Olympic Games. Hair was long, dropping out was all the rage, so-called soul surfing was supreme and the sport and industry in California had choked on their excesses. While the art of riding a wave continued to develop, it wasn't with the same pace and intensity of the Nat Young/Bob McTavish period of the late 1960s. Surfers were content to cruise in search of uncrowded waves and they were certainly in no hurry to promote their recreation as a mainstream sport.

Yet with this unlikely backdrop, professional surfing was born and in 1976 International Professional Surfing (IPS), controlled by Hawaiian contest promoter Fred Hemmings, strung together 12 events in Hawaii, Australia, South Africa, New Zealand and Florida and called it a professional circuit. Peter Townend, a small, blond surfer from the Gold Coast, had accumulated enough points by the end of the year to be crowned the first world champion in an inauspicious and enormously unpublicised ceremony in Honolulu. Through consistently high placings, Townend had done enough to take the title; for the first time surfing had a world champion who hadn't actually won a contest. Mark Richards was already part of this circuit called professional surfing but, unlike a hardy few pioneers, he had no intention of taking out a bank loan to chase the fledgling and unremunerative tour.

Mark Richards was happy to compete at home in Australia and in his beloved Hawaii, where he would go anyway to ride its big winter surf. He still believed his contest successes were merely an adjunct to his real career, which was making surfboards. What he and his fellow professionals wanted to do most of all was go surfing. They fashioned their lives around the sport they loved. It was a most welcome bonus if they could actually be paid for doing it. To this day Mark Richards is still remarkably free of mercenary instincts. A surfboard, hand shaped by Mark Richards, four times world champion, will cost a customer no more than most professionally-made boards: 'I'm sure some people would be prepared to pay extra for my boards but I'm not prepared to cash in on my name like that. I wouldn't be comfortable doing it.'

In the northern winter of 1978–79 Mark had another enjoyable stint in Hawaii, further developing his twin fin boards but having no great impact on the contests. He still managed to finish the year ranked 10th in the world behind new world champion Wayne Bartholomew. Back in Australia he lined up for the three-contest autumn circuit, which consisted of the Stubbies at Burleigh Heads in Queensland, the Rip Curl/Quiksilver event at Bells Beach in Victoria and the rich Surfabout in Sydney.

In the IPS events the top 16 seeds went straight into the main event where they met qualifiers from the trials and often several wildcards. Unlike the contests of today, where surfers are rigidly seeded according to rankings, the draw for the early events was made by pulling surfers' names from a hat and matching a qualifier with one of the top 16, regardless of the seed's ranking or where the qualifier had finished in the trials. This often led to ridiculous first-round confrontations between surfers who under a seeding system would not have been drawn against each other until much later in the contest.

On the surface of it the pairing of Mark Richards, ranked 10th in 1978, and Larry Bertleman, ranked 51st, should have been about right in the first round of the 1979 Stubbies. But twin-fin rider Bertleman's lowly ranking was a result more of his absence from much of the 1978 tour than any lack of ability and as Mark remembers: 'Nobody wanted to draw Larry Bertleman because everyone was terrified he would pull off one of his 360-degree turns which he had been perfecting and the judges would go ga-ga and score him up. So apparently the look on my face told the story when the organisers pulled our names out of the hat to meet in the first round. Michael Tomson wrote in *Surfing* magazine that I looked like I was going to choke on my orange juice.

'That was the heat of the contest. It was like a final but it was in the first round. It was very intense. The drop-in rule was pretty vague in those days and I more or less dropped in on him but he had no chance of making the wave. But he protested because technically it was a drop-in and it was very nearly upheld. And when you win a tough heat you don't want to have to re-surf it.'

Mark's confidence soared after defeating Bertleman and he went on to beat teenager Cheyne Horan in the final. 'That was another of those contests where I felt really good. I think my fitness level was probably at its peak, though I never was as fit as I should have been, and I felt my surfing was on another level. It wasn't that I was so much better than the other guys, it was just that I had a board that was so much better and allowed me to do so much more on a wave. I felt I had this advanced piece of equipment and the other guys were riding pre-historic single fins. My boards were light, and fast and so manoeuvrable. I felt I had such a huge advantage that as long as I got the waves I was unbeatable.'

After losing to Burleigh experts Michael Peterson in the 1977 final and Wayne Bartholomew in the 1978 semi-finals, Mark Richards was now Stubbies champion. The circuit then moved to Bells Beach where in small, wind-blown surf Richards again beat Bartholomew in the final. On 1 April, he even pocketed $500 by winning an invitation-only Expression Session sponsored by board maker Terry Fitzgerald at Dee Why Beach in Sydney. As journalist Phil Jarratt wrote in *Surfing* magazine, the only real interest left in the Australian circuit was seeing if Richards could make it a clean sweep in the Surfabout.

Coca-Cola and 2SM had given the job of tournament director of Surfabout to Englishman Paul Holmes, the editor of *Tracks* magazine and later to become editor of *Surfing* before moving on to a senior position with a surf clothing company. Holmes had had stunning success with Surfabout the previous year when Sydney's northern beaches were blessed with excellent waves and the final was an epic encounter at North Steyne between winner Larry Blair, who had qualified from the trials, and Wayne Lynch.

Surfabout was packaged largely for television. It had a waiting period and was moveable so the chance of getting good waves were high. At the start of the 1979 Surfabout, nobody had an inkling just how far Holmes was prepared to go in search of good waves. But when, with 16 surfers still left in the event, the surf in Sydney went flat and showed no signs of improving, Holmes airlifted the entire contest to Bells Beach, which had big, cold and highly contestable waves. Mark Richards beat his friend from Hawaii, Bobby Owens, in the heats but the unthinkable happened in the quarter-finals when, with victory over Cheyne Horan well within reach, Mark fell off a wave he believes would have clinched the heat. 'It was like shock, horror, MR fell off. I never fall off.'

Apart from losing this unexpected way, Mark has other less-than-fond memories of this historic contest: 'I was really pissed off they went to Bells. I didn't want to be there. I had a really bad attitude about moving the contest. I wanted to be in Sydney. As much as I liked the Bells contests, there were two things I didn't like about the place. One was the cold, especially after coming from the warm water at Burleigh, and the other was the mud. I was never confident at Bells that I wasn't going to slip off. Before they tarred the carpark you would get this red mud on your feet and no matter how hard you tried it seemed you could never get it off.

'I have always looked after my boards. You take particular care if you have made something yourself. You have that special pride. So you can imagine how I felt when I got my boards out of the aeroplane at the airport down there and found they had been dinged because they had been thrown in with all the camera gear willy nilly. The moment I was knocked out I said I'm outta here. Take me home. It was completely the wrong attitude. A professional athlete should make the best of whatever is available.'

Losing and Mark Richards don't mix, according to his wife Jenny. 'It was very hard being around him after he lost a heat, especially if he thought he had won. He became very quiet and withdrawn and there was no point in trying to cheer him up. It was just a waste of time. You had to let him come out of it by himself. There was one time in particular when he lost at Bells to Simon Anderson on an interference that was a very tough decision. They were on the same wave but nowhere near each other. Mark was just furious. Furious with himself, furious with the judges, furious with the system. I had to shut up and keep out of the way.'

That year for the first time the world tour included Japan, where four small events attracted all the leading contenders. Mark's main reason for going to Japan was not so much to consolidate his lead but to keep faith with his Japanese sponsor who was paying him $US1000 a year to sell Richards-endorsed surfboards and clothing. 'He was supposed to pay me a percentage of anything he sold over a certain mark but it seemed he always sold the bare minimum. I asked to see the records but they were in Japanese so I had no way of telling what was going on. Anyhow, I thought a thousand dollars a year was phenomenal.' Mark Richards was young, naive and managerless. Extraordinarily loose arrangements between sponsor and surfer are still the norm in professional surfing.

It was a month of intense competition in the small Japanese waves, but Mark also recalls the great hospitality of their hosts and the highly enjoyable and fascinating times he had away from the surf. But while the Japanese were friendly toward the surfers, there was at times no love lost among the surfers.

The program began with victory for Mark. In the semi-finals at Niijima he had beaten Cheyne Horan after Horan had paddled into the beach because he thought he saw a shark. Much to Mark's disgust the heat was extended by five minutes, but Horan was unable to catch up. 'One of the Japanese magazines carried a story that Cheyne Horan had paddled in because he saw a shark but what he really saw was Mark Richards in a yellow wetsuit,' Mark recalls.

In the final Mark faced old adversary Michael Ho, a confrontation that had an interesting sidelight. Tension had begun to build between what were the two main camps on the professional tour. In one corner were the Hawaiians, with Michael Ho, Larry Bertleman, Dane Kealoha, Hans Hedemann, Buzzy Kerbox and Reno Abellira. In the other corner were the Australians and South Africans, just as combative in the water but perhaps less clannish. Mark recalls much cheering and jeering from Ho's supporters during the final and he found the intensity of the barracking a little bewildering. 'Apparently the Aussies and the South Africans just got jack of their bias and went down on the beach in front of them and just dropped their daks and threw them the big brown eye. Imagine that happening at a contest now?'

The Japanese tour was a good earner for Mark as he posted a first, a second and two fifths to consolidate his lead on the rankings. The contests were also encouraging signs of how strong Japanese support for professional surfing would become. Mark also found the atmosphere conducive: 'All the events were held in atrocious conditions but they were really well run and people turned out in thousands to watch. There were people all over the beach and the autograph hunting was insane. They wanted surfers to sign everything from their bodies, clothes, to their cars, to car seats, books, magazines, all sorts of things. We all felt like sports stars.

'All the sponsors had organised promotional tours for the surfers in between the contests. They would advertise that such and such surfers would be at a certain surf shop at a certain time and when we arrived there would be hundreds of Japanese kids getting autographs and taking photos.'

Mark's sponsor, who also had Shaun Tomson and Reno Abellira on his team, was the grand master of these promotions. At one such function, a surfing movie preview, 'Shaun, Reno and I were the honoured guests. It was done in this huge auditorium and before the film started they had the three of us on stage. They interviewed us, with Doji Isaka [Japan's lone representative at the 1970 world titles in Victoria] acting as interpreter and then we had to actually give a surfing demonstration right there on the stage. Shaun did this thing where he described surfing Jeffreys Bay in South Africa and Reno described surfing Sunset Beach in Hawaii. And I told them about surfing in the Stubbies at Burleigh Heads in machine-like perfect tubes. I'm crouched down on the stage demonstrating how you ride the tube and Doji had this idea of getting the Japanese people who were up on the stage to simulate a tube. They stood over me with their arms out and there was I crouched under this human tube. And the audience just went batty. They had ridden Jeffreys with Shaun, Sunset with Reno and now they were in the tube with me at Burleigh and they loved it. They were clapping and cheering and hooting. It was totally bizarre.'

Mark emerged from Japan as a clear leader on the ratings and although the circuit's next stop was South Africa, which now hosted a second tournament, the Hang Ten, in addition to the durable Gunston 500, he went back to Australia and work in the shaping bay: 'I remember Ian [Cairns] asking me if I was going to South Africa and I had said no, probably not. I still had this thing about being a shaper. Pro surfing to me was just a sideline, shaping was going to be the career. And really in the years before, PT [Townend], Shaun [Tomson] and Rabbit [Bartholomew] hadn't derived any gigantic financial reward from being world champion. There was no pot of gold at the end of the rainbow and though it sounds strange I had no desire to continue on, even though I was in the lead.'

Cairns told Richards he would be silly to skip the rest of the tour. All he needed to do was turn up, get through a heat or two and he was a cinch for the title. He could be champion of the world. Cairns, one of the finest big-wave riders Australia has produced, is a big, well-spoken man who can put forward a well-reasoned, cogent argument in a forceful way. Still Mark demurred, and went back to Newcastle.

He watched his lead disintegrate as Kealoha won in Durban and New Jersey and Bartholomew won in Florida. Coming into the final two-contest Hawaiian leg he appeared to have given his chief rivals too much leeway. Kealoha boosted his chances by placing second to Australian Larry Blair in the final of the Pipeline Masters but Richards made up ground on Horan and Bartholomew by placing fourth in the Masters after the other two Australians had made earlier exits.

So now it was all down to the World Cup at Haleiwa with four surfers in with a chance, the remotest being Mark

Richards. But, in one dramatic day of competition, with just 16 surfers left in the Cup, in solid 6ft to 8ft surf it all fell into place for Mark Richards. Bartholomew was the first to go. He was eliminated in his first round, knocked out by qualifier Ken Bradshaw in what was a huge upset. Bradshaw, a big-wave devotee, had no great contest record. On form in this size surf he should have been thrashed by Bartholomew, but the reigning world champion had a poor heat, breaking a leg rope and spending much of the heat swimming. He gave Bradshaw a huge start but even though the Hawaiian failed to capitalise fully on his good fortune, Bartholomew still couldn't peg him back. Out went Bartholomew to finish third in the world title race.

In the same round the next challenger to depart was Dane Kealoha, who was a raging hot favourite to beat Puerto Rican qualifier Edwin Santos. But in a strategic bungle, Kealoha wasted too much time waiting for the big outside waves as Santos racked up several good rides on the smaller, inside waves. The big sets didn't come and a wave-starved Kealoha was eliminated. Meanwhile, Mark Richards was keeping his hopes alive with wins over Hawaiian Mark Liddell and South African Michael Tomson. Horan surfed brilliantly to reach the semi-finals where he ran into wily campaigner Peter Townend. Townend, the 1976 world champion, was displeased with Horan for quitting the Bronzed Aussies surf team Townend had formed with Ian Cairns and Mark Warren. So perhaps there was a little more intensity in his hustling as he put unbearable pressure on the hapless Horan and went in to the final against Mark Richards. But Horan, who had been runner-up to Bartholomew the previous year, could still win the world title if Townend could beat Richards in the final. Mark remembers the day vividly: 'When the day began I felt no pressure because I was lying fourth and the odds of Dane and Rabbit going out so early against people like Santos and Bradshaw were astronomical. But as the day wore on I realised I had a glimmer of hope but I still knew that all Cheyne had to do was make the final. It was all happening so quickly, it was a blur, and I was trying not to think about it. I was trying to keep away the thought of what might be. Then all of a sudden it came down to the final after the unthinkable had happened yet again with Cheyne being beaten at just the right time and again it was an unlikely result. Before the final I was very nervous, particularly because I was against Peter and I had seen how he had beaten Cheyne in the semi. I was worried Peter would work me over in the wave catching department and beat me that way. I knew wave for wave I could win but Peter's hustling ability frightened me. And sure enough, after both of us had caught a few waves he went for the inside, and in those days the golden rule in competition was not to surrender the inside position. I was prepared to paddle to Sunset Beach if necessary rather than let him through. So we ended up sitting way out past the break, nowhere near where the waves were breaking, and I was determined not to give up the inside because that would give him first choice of the next set and would leave the way open for me to be an easy target for intimidation in future competition. I felt Peter had a slight lead so after 10 minutes I realised there was no point in sitting on him any longer because I would lose so I paddled back into the line-up and immediately picked up a wave. However, because I was so nervous and rattled by this stage and I knew the world title was on the line, I fell on a couple of waves. The pressure was getting to me. Coming out of the water I didn't feel confident.'

The most nervous spectator on the beach that day was

Mark's girlfriend Jenny Jobson, who had flown in from Australia. 'Because I was teaching I couldn't leave Australia until the beginning of the school holidays. I only flew into Hawaii on the last day of the World Cup and had no idea what was happening at Haleiwa. Because Mark was competing, his friend Tony Higa had to pick me up from the airport. We went straight to the beach and when we arrived, Mark was already out in the water for the final with Peter Townend. People told us that if Mark won he would win the world championship. It was the most exciting heat.'

Jenny watched anxiously and with some frustration as the tactical duel developed. 'Mark's a very stubborn person. In those days with no priority buoy as they now have in two-man heats, Mark would never give up the inside. I thought "You stubborn bastard, you are going to lose this heat and the world championship". I actually think he was prepared to lose the world title rather than give up the inside.' She was confident Mark could beat Townend on surfing ability and when the combatants finally got down to some surfing, she thought Mark had done just enough to win.

Mark took the World Cup and the world surfing title he never planned to win. Now he knew what it was like to be number one, to be recognised officially as the best. 'It was a great feeling, I really liked it. I thought this has got something going for it after all. I decided very soon after winning the world title that I would definitely go after it for a second time.' But the fanfare heralding his remarkable feat was less than deafening. After collecting his cheque he walked unhindered back to Jenny on the beach. Today's mandatory multi-media conference was still a dream away. 'There may have been a TV interview and a few people patted me on the back,' Mark recalls. A night or two later Mark and Jenny went to a function at Steamers restaurant

Mark and Jenny together
in the mid-1980s. 'We
knew we would eventually
get married but we were
not in any hurry,' says
Jenny.

in the small town of Haleiwa for the world title presentation. His mementoes were a Rolex watch and a small plaque inscribed with a Pan Am logo. There was no cash prize, no air tickets, no sponsor's bonus. *Surfing* magazine did pay tribute to the sport's new champion, naming him surfer of the year and going to great expense to commission leading rock photographer Norman Seef to shoot a portrait of Mark for the cover. '*Surfing* thought that what I had done warranted for the first time putting just a face on the cover instead of an action shot. I turned up at [Norman's] studios on Sunset Boulevarde in Los Angeles and he said "Put a wetsuit on because we're going to drench you". At about 5pm we went out on to Sunset Boulevarde and he had me standing there, in a yellow wetsuit and with a pink surfboard under my arm, pretending to hitch a ride. I didn't get a lift but I sure got a lot of funny stares.'

Jenny recalls watching amusedly as Mark went through this bizarre ritual to a surprising number of shouts of encouragement from Los Angelinos who recognised Mark. 'Yo, MR', was yelled from quite a few cars inching along on the freeway that strange afternoon.

Mark Richards, world surfing champion, had stepped into the ranks of the full-time professionals. History beckoned.

After Mark won the 1979 World Cup, *Surfing* magazine commissioned rock photographer Norman Seef to photograph him on the streets of Los Angeles. PHOTO: SURFING MAGAZINE

CHAPTER FIVE

IN DEFENCE
OF THE CROWN

I t may have been official that Mark Richards was world number one at the start of the 1980 International Professional Surfing season but there was still plenty of debate as to who was the best surfer.

Many people believed that Dane Kealoha, who made a late charge but faltered in the last event in 1979, was the greatest surfer. A big, muscular Hawaiian with a driving, aggressive style, Kealoha became an early target for Mark in 1980. It wasn't that he thought Kealoha was a better surfer — he didn't — it was that he quickly realised Kealoha had a competitive act that would impress the judges: 'By this stage Dane was also on twin fins and he could really make them move. He wasn't doing as many manoeuvres as most of the other surfers but he could generate incredible speed. It was great to watch,' Mark recalls.

Kealoha's backhand surfing, particularly in hollow waves, was also strong. He had perfected a move where he could compress his body and keep his board at the tightest angle to ride in the tube backside. While acknowledging Kealoha's expertise, Mark showed no false modesty when he told *Surfer* magazine at the time: 'The guy's brilliant but I think I can beat him easily. I'm just the better surfer. Dane has all the technical ability but his mind is letting him down. He's gradually overcoming it but he still makes some radical mistakes.'

Kealoha, Richards, Horan, Bartholomew and Tomson were the dominant surfers of the late 1970s and early 1980s. While the other four continued well into the 1980s, and 1990s in Horan's case, Kealoha quit the tour after the 1983 season, the first year it was controlled by the Association of Surfing Professionals (ASP), which had taken over from International Professional Surfing. He was extremely disenchanted with an ASP ruling that surfers ranked in the top 16 could not compete in non-rated events, which meant that he would have to forgo contests in Hawaii such as the prestigious Duke Kahanamoku Classic. Kealoha, who had tour finishes of 9, 4, 2, 3, 6 and 14 from 1978 to 1983, is still regarded as one of the better surfers in Hawaii.

Perhaps smarting from his defeat in home waters in 1979, Kealoha began his 1980 campaign in spectacular fashion in Australia. He reached successive finals at Cronulla and Burleigh Heads and lost them both to Bartholomew and Gold Coast recreational surfer Peter Harris, in controversial circumstances. Although recalling that the final with Bartholomew was hellishly close, Mark thinks Kealoha should have beaten Harris in the Stubbies because he believes Harris was overscored for a tube ride that drew thunderous applause.

Significantly, Kealoha had beaten Mark in the semi-finals of both events. 'I always made a point after losing a heat to shake the hand of the other surfer and congratulate him. When I did that to Dane after those two heats he replied "Don't worry, you're still the world champion".' But being the world champion didn't matter in that context. All that mattered was to beat Dane. Mark was right on Kealoha's hammer going into the third event at Bells and finally beat Kealoha in small waves in the Bells semi-finals. 'By then I had figured out what he was doing and I just decided to go flat out, to go as fast as I could, to cut back on manoeuvres and match him for speed. I just scraped past him in that one.' For the third year in a row, Mark beat Bartholomew in the final.

In the last contest of the Australian leg, the Surfabout at North Narrabeen, Mark went out in the quarter-finals to Wollongong youngster Chris ('Critta') Byrne, who later lost the final to Hawaiian Buzzy Kerbox. Byrne, youngest brother of leading surfer and surfboard maker Phil Byrne, had been making a serious tilt at the professional circuit. One of the youngest on the professional circuit, Critta moved from 15th in 1978 to eighth by the end of 1980. But tragically it all ended here when a serious back complaint cut short his promising career. Mark says that Chris Byrne 'was a hard guy to beat. He was probably the most aggressive guy I have surfed against in a competitive situation. He never gave an inch. It was really physical when you were surfing against Critta. It's hard to tell how far he would have gone. If intensity and desire count for anything he had 100 per cent. It's an unknown quantity when someone bails out with a problem. It's pretty fair to assume he wouldn't have gone backwards. He would have only gone forward.'

By the end of the four-event Australian leg Mark was leading the ratings and focusing unswervingly on keeping his title. To this end he altered his strategy radically. For the first time he decided to chase contests in the world circuit. In 1980 that meant going to South Africa, site of the Gunston and Hang Ten in Durban. 'Before I went to South

Africa, I didn't even think about the political situation.[*] At that age I knew nothing about it anyway. I wasn't politically aware. I just went there to surf. As I got a bit older I gave it more thought. So for me it was a case of I'm off to surf in South Africa in the contests. That's probably a really self-centred thought on the whole thing but I think it's the way surfing makes you.

'When you're young things such as politics, responsibilities, fairness in life don't mean anything. It's just me, me, me. But after a couple of trips to South Africa I flashed on just how unfair the whole system was and how unequally the blacks were treated. I thought to myself, "This is pretty strange. It's all because of a different skin colour. There is something really wrong here."

'I don't think the sporting boycotts had much effect on change in South Africa. I think it was more the economic boycott, the big corporations pulling out of South Africa, that had the effect. It struck me when I was there that the people of English descent were willing to change but that the people of Afrikaner descent weren't. And it seemed really odd to me that the Afrikaners base their belief in their superiority over the blacks in their interpretation of what the Bible says. It seems to me that apartheid goes against all God's teaching, that it's alien to the idea of loving your fellow men, of all people being equal. But there was never much point in talking to South Africans about apartheid because for them it was accepted practice. It was normal, it was the way they had been brought up. Some South Africans I spoke to were amazed that we in Australia didn't have servants, that we didn't have people to do all the work around the house and that we did it ourselves. The changes

[*] Mark was blacklisted by the United Nations for participating in a sports event held in South Africa.

there have been good but there's a still a long way to go and there are still a lot of people who have no intention of sharing power with the blacks.'

Mark remembers his first visit to South Africa with great fondness. The professional surfers, and particularly Mark as reigning world champion, were welcomed warmly in Durban, the port and resort city on the Natal coast. Huge crowds jammed the beach and the surfers were mobbed by autograph hunters and young South African surfers eager to talk to their heroes. Contest organiser Peter Burness ran the events with precision and flair, introducing such things as losers' rounds and best-of-three sets right through the contest.

Mark's lasting memory of the trip is not the fact that he won both events or that he rode excellent waves at Jeffreys Bay and on the Natal south coast, but how well he surfed. He thinks that during that month in South Africa he surfed about as well as he ever had and he felt totally invincible, especially as the contests were held in good right handers with clean, open faces, tailor-made for his carving, swooping style. 'The surf was so rippable. It was perfect for my twin fin. I think I reached the peak of my competitive achievement in South Africa. I've seen footage of those contests and my surfing is pretty futuristic stuff compared with the other guys. I had my twinnies at the peak of their design. I had one that was 6ft 4in, it was the one with a blue rail and a green rail and an orange deck and that was the best board I ever made.'

His surfing was clinically accurate yet at the same time expressive and avant garde. Leading South African surfer Paul Naude wrote: 'It became embarrassingly apparent that Richards is so far ahead of everyone else in this game of surfing that it's ridiculous.'

You would expect such a superb athlete to work hard on his fitness, but Mark's regimen during his stay in Durban would horrify the health-conscious professionals of the 1990s. He would surf in the morning and afternoon, and relax in between with a Wilbur Smith novel as he swigged Coca-Cola and ate a family-size bar of Caramello chocolate. Dinner was steak and chips. 'I don't think I ate a green vegetable or a piece of fruit for a month. I don't think I was ever very fit throughout my whole career. I used to get very tired and there were times when my lack of fitness probably cost me heats because I didn't have the energy to catch the right waves. And sometimes on waves toward the end of the heat my legs would get very sore, particularly at the long point breaks such as Durban, Bells and Burleigh, and I'd be thinking "I can't do another turn. My legs are killing me." So I wouldn't finish the wave off the way I may have liked. In the early days we thought surfing was enough exercise. There was no way you would do any stretching exercises before you went in the water the way so many surfers do now. It would have been considered very uncool.'

By the end of the South African season Mark, who also had joined up with Cheyne Horan and Wayne Bartholomew to win an international teams event, had won three of the seven events on tour and held a commanding lead on the ratings. He decided to miss the contest in Brazil, but iced the cake in Hawaii by winning the Pipeline Masters and coming third after Ian Cairns and Michael Ho in the World Cup in monster surf at Haleiwa.

During the Pipeline Masters, Mark experienced one of the few ugly incidents of his competitive career. On one particular wave Kealoha took off in front of Mark but quickly pulled out. But Mark eventually had to straighten out over the shallow reef when another Hawaiian, Kainoa Downing, dropped down in front of him on what had been an excellent right-hander at Backdoor Pipeline. Downing was totally in the wrong, but he angrily challenged Mark to fight and even wanted to go on with the argument physically on the beach after the final. He was restrained by his father George and brother Keone. Downing finished last in that final while Richards won the world championship by a record number of points: 'It was very satisfying to win it again. I had achieved a goal. Many times you set yourself goals and you don't reach them but at the start of 1980 I had made it pretty clear I wanted to keep the world title. But it's really hard to describe that feeling of winning. It's like when someone wins a contest and they're asked how they feel and they say "Great" but great doesn't really describe it. Relief, accomplishment, it's all sorts of things rolled into one.' More than ever Mark Richards' surfing became the standard by which others were judged.

Mark now had solid sponsorship from Lightning Bolt surf clothing company and Victory wetsuits, his exposure in the surfing and non-surfing media was huge, he was able to afford smart cars and he had money in the bank. It was at this point that Mark Richards was at his most potent and his most vulnerable. If ever he were going to be sidetracked or seduced by the trappings of success it would have been midway through his four-year world championship reign. Many other great sportspeople have had their focus blurred by the attendant fame and glory.

For Mark Richards it didn't happen. The man is extraordinary and at the same time ordinary. As much as he enjoyed a 'nice amount of fame', Mark never set out to be different, to be noticed, to be praised. Pare away the trophies, the money, the fame and you constantly return to a young boy who at some indeterminate point realised that what he wanted to do in his life more than anything else in the world was surf. Many people around the world saw Mark surf brilliantly to win many contests and collect riches and fame. They saw him in movies and read about him in magazines and newspapers. But over the years a privileged few in Newcastle have witnessed the world champion, the greatest and best known surfer in the world, paddle out into huge waves at Merewether Beach and surf them with abandon and skill all by himself. For Richards and for some of us who watched, these are great moments. It's unlikely that many other sportspeople would look back on their career and treasure moments of such solitude, away from judges, opponents, crowds. Away from the circus and the public arena. By their very nature most sports require these things. But surfing is different and it's worth considering that had Mark Richards never made a career out of what he loved to do, he and just about every other great surfer still would have pursued their goals to surf as much and as well as they could.

When the tour began in 1981 all eyes were on Mark Richards, a happy, healthy man almost 25 years old who had the world at his feet. By then he had settled into a groove. His mission in life had become to compete on the world tour, not shape surfboards, and to win the world title. 'By then I was thinking records. I had already won the world title twice. Nobody had done that before but it was conceivable that someone else could win it twice so I was thinking maybe I could win it three times, which may not ever be done again.'

Event number one in 1981 was the Stubbies, which was held in micro-surf at Burleigh Heads before an enormous crowd. Mark got his campaign off to a great start by beating Kealoha yet again, in a final where both surfers were riding over almost exposed rocks. Val Richards waited on the shore with a spare board just in case he ripped a fin out: 'The Stubbies was very exciting. It was always packed out with people. Some girls used to come up from Coffs Harbour and they were Mark's fan club. One of their fathers had a manchester store and they had this huge yellow beach towel that they would drape over the face of the cliff with a huge MR emblem in the middle of it. They had MR shirts, MR this and that. They came for a few years.'

Robert August, a great Californian surfer of the 1960s and star of the definitive surf movie, *The Endless Summer*, said the great attraction of contests for him was the chance to meet girls. Mark appears not to have seized the obvious advantages of being a famous, revered sporting champion travelling around the world. For a start he was not really a social animal: 'I guess I'm a chip off the old block in that regard. My father detested going out. When I was in Hawaii I'd spend most nights at home or I would go around to Bernie Baker's and watch television. Plus for most of the time I was on the tour I was going out with Jenny. That's just about the only relationship I've had.' Mark Warren, now a successful television sports presenter in Sydney, was the usual fierce opponent but also one of Mark's staunch friends: 'The groupy thing never really touched Mark. It didn't get to him. He'd just giggle in that gawky way of his when he realised someone was paying attention to him.'

As Jenny Richards explains: 'Mark's a loner. Quite often he didn't go out and celebrate after a contest because we had to move on to another one the next day. But he's never been into drinking or drugs, he hates dancing and he hates going to night clubs because they're so smoky and you can't have a conversation because the music is so loud. He also feels very conspicuous because people stare at him. I'm a social person and I have a group of girlfriends. Practically any social contact we have now is initiated by me. Mark's celebration was to sit down in front of the TV and eat a bar of chocolate. It's his idea of heaven. Still is. When he won the Stubbies we were staying with his parents at Rainbow Bay so we all just went home and had dinner and said "That's nice, Mark won today". He's like his father. Ray was a loner and Val was a social person who liked going with her friends and they were very happy together. This might sound funny but I was genuinely surprised Ray came to our wedding. He got dressed up in a suit and tie. If it hadn't been his only son I don't think he would have come.'

From waves under 1ft high at Burleigh Heads the professionals moved down to Bells Beach in Victoria where on one day of the Easter contest the waves reached a near-perfect 15ft. Apart from the size of its waves, the 1981 Bells Beach contest was momentous because it was the first time a surfer had won a major event on a surfboard with three fins. The winner was Simon Anderson, a laconic, genial surfer from that remarkable spawning ground of talent, North Narrabeen. Anderson is a radical, powerful and stylish surfer, whose control makes everything look simple. His mien in and out of the water is that of the cavalier Aussie bloke. He won the Australian junior titles in 1971 and 1972, and in 1977 he pulled off the remarkable feat of winning both the Bells and Coke contests. The Coke event that year was held in barely contestable tiny waves yet this hulking man of well over 6ft and 15 stone found enough speed in the atrocious waves to win. Because of his relaxed yet aggressive style, and his sheer size, he earned a reputation as a big-wave specialist as the West Australian giant Ian Cairns had done before him, yet both men were also extremely adept in the most marginal of conditions. There are not many more pleasing sights in surfing than watching Simon Anderson, body erect and arms akimbo, carving savagely through big left handers at his favoured North Narrabeen.

A leading board shaper, Anderson had had trouble coming to terms with the twin-fin design popularised by Mark Richards so he set about experimenting with new shapes. What he came up with was a three-fin surfboard called the thruster, which enhanced a surfboard's manoeuvrability without sacrificing its ability to 'grip' the wave face. Although he didn't know it at the time, Anderson revolutionised the surfboard industry. By the mid-1980s, virtually every surfboard manufactured had three fins. Single fins and twin fins were obsolete. The thruster now brought high performance surfing within the scope of a far greater number of surfers. Because they make surfing so much easier — or less difficult — the thrusters have narrowed the gap between the elite professionals and the competent recreational surfer. There have been many subtle variations made to surfboard design since, but nobody has produced a viable alternative to the three-fin board. Simon Anderson must take his place with people such as Californian Bob Simmons, who made 'super light' boards out of foam in the early 1950s, and Bob McTavish, who reduced the length of surfboards by about a third, among the great surfboard designers in the sport's history.

Bells Beach, Easter Saturday, 1981, was one of the great days in Australian surfing history. The superb reef break just near the small town of Torquay had not been this big for the annual contest since 1965, when local hero Terry Wall, now a Newcastle neighbour of Richards, almost drowned in huge surf. Mark Richards pulled into the car park early in the morning on the day of the contest. It was cold and grey and the wind was howling offshore and the surf was huge. 'I can't recall if anybody was out but AC/DC's

Launching into the unknown: Mark Richards surfs Off the Wall, Hawaii 1978.
PHOTO: BERNIE BAKER-LEONARD BRADY/ISLAND STYLE

Jamming at Off the Wall, Hawaii, 1978. The 1977/78 season in Hawaii ushered in a new era, with Richards using his revolutionary twin fin boards. PHOTO: BERNIE BAKER-LEONARD BRADY/ISLAND STYLE

Narrabeen Beach, Australia, 1979: Richards applies his rip, slash and tear approach.
PHOTO: PETER CRAWFORD

"Hells Bells" was blaring over the loudspeaker. I don't know if it was coincidence or somebody had put it on deliberately. I had my "big-wave board" in the car. It was a 6ft 4in twin fin. I was riding a 6ft 2in twin fin in those days and this may seem stupid now but my big-wave board was only two inches longer. If I had had my choice I would have taken out a 7ft 4in board or longer. A lot of the local surfers were auctioning off their big single fins in the car park to the contestants. The heats were for 45 minutes and we were allowed to start paddling out 30 minutes before the start. The trick was to jump off the point, get bashed by the white water, drift across the bay and hopefully you would be close enough to the spot where you could make it through to paddle like crazy before another set came. I've had some big days at Merewether but that was probably the biggest and most lined up surf I have ever had in Australia. The thing that struck me about that surf was that it was probably as awesome as some of the waves I have ridden in Hawaii. The waves that day were comparable in size and power to many of the waves in Hawaii. At most places in Hawaii, with the exception of Waimea Bay, the waves come in big peaks but on that day at Bells the waves were incredibly lined up, like Waimea. You could see this huge wall coming from way down the coast and it was as though we were catching the tail end of these freight trains. It was huge. I survived on my 6ft 4in twin fin. I was nursing it off the bottom but it's amazing how you can make do with what you've got. If you really want to catch a wave you can catch it on anything.'
Mark reached the quarter-finals, which were held in much smaller waves, but he lost to eventual runner-up Cheyne Horan. It was Simon Anderson who triumphed at Bells 1981 as Mark relates: 'Simon's win was badly reported. All the stories came out that Simon had won Bells on his new-

fangled thruster in 12 to 15ft surf, which isn't really correct. Simon surfed the best on the big day, he surfed unbelieveably, but the thing I think was Simon's greatest achievement was not his big-wave surfing but the fact that he beat Cheyne [Horan], who was fantastic in small surf, in 2ft to 4ft surf at Rincon a few days later. I felt that Simon's great achievement was to back up after his extraordinary performance on the big day to beat Cheyne in the small waves.'

Next stop on the tour was the Surfabout, held in marvellous waves before big crowds over three days at North Narrabeen. A young trials qualifier from Norah Head called Glen Winton drew Mark in round one and took a fearful beating as Richards posted the highest score of what was a day of high performance surfing. Three years earlier at North Narrabeen Mark had gone in as raging hot favourite against qualifier Jim Banks, a teenager from Cronulla, in similar conditions at North Narrabeen in round one of the 1978 Surfabout: 'I had that heat well and truly in the palm of my hand until Banksy got a five-second tube ride and that was that. The defeat was still fresh in my mind when I took on Glen but I seemed to get all the good waves and he didn't get any tubes and I won easily.' A man who takes success and failure with smiling equanimity, Winton went on to become one of Australia's truly great professional surfers.

Despite just about every wave ridden during the three days of competition being a left hander, the final eight surfers were all natural footers. Mark believes that the 1981 Surfabout heralded the adoption of a new style of backside tube riding to counter high scores posted by surfers riding hollow waves on their forehand. Various attempts had been made by people such as Shaun and Michael Tomson, Dane Kealoha and Wayne Bartholomew in Pipeline's big lefts, but at North Narrabeen Kealoha and Anderson showed how it could be done in smaller waves. Kealoha had a very effective method where he leaned forward and held both rails of his board. This manoeuvre is still very much in vogue and is called the 'pig dog'. Anderson fitted his mighty frame inside the small tubes by squatting and lying back into the wall, a move too difficult for most surfers. But it worked for Anderson and he went on to replicate his 1977 feat of back-to-back Bells and Surfabout victories, beating in the final Shaun Tomson, who had despatched Mark in the semi-finals.

After an unproductive first trip to Bali, also the first stop on the Indonesian island for the IPS tour, Mark went to South Africa where he was ninth in the Gunston and first in the Mainstay Magnum. At this stage the professional tour was taking whatever sponsorship they could get and the sponsors for the two contests were a tobacco firm and a liquor manufacturer. Now some contests are sponsored by government-funded, anti-drug and anti-drink drives.

On his second trip to South Africa, Mark saw for the first time the amazing surfing of Martin Potter, a fifteen-year-old Englishman whose family had migrated to Zimbabwe (then called Rhodesia) before moving on to Durban. Potter, the 1989 world champion, went on to become an all-time great but when the professional tour hit Durban in the southern winter of 1981 he was just a relatively obscure but talented youngster riding a Richards-designed twin fin. Not long before the South African events, Potter had been the highest scorer in a scholastics clash between South Africa and the United States. Third in that event was Tom Curren. In an amazing few weeks Potter beat some of the leading surfers of the day to reach the finals of both contests, before losing to Horan in the Gunston and then to Richards in the Mainstay Magnum.

Three champions: Mark Richards (left) with Cheyne Horan (centre) and Wayne Bartholemew (right). PHOTO: NEWS LIMITED

Though he had won one of the South African events Richards had still surrendered the lead on the ratings to Horan and he was a worried man. He was anxious to hang on to his world title and he was getting frustrated at the push for Horan in both the surfing and non-surfing media. He felt perhaps the search had begun for a new leader and that Cheyne Horan was the heir apparent.

So the reluctant traveller cashed in his return ticket to Australia and followed the tour to Brazil. The Waimea 500 was held at Prainha Beach near Rio De Janeiro in tiny waves and Horan increased his ratings lead by riding to victory on a board he had had made specially for the terrible conditions.[*] Richards finished third to keep the pressure on Horan and then smartly headed back to his beloved Newcastle.

It wasn't long before he was back on the road again, this time for the first IPS-rated event to be held on the US west coast. The US Pro was held at the classic right hand point break of Malibu, perhaps the beach most associated with modern surfing and the only beach with a type of surfboard named after it. Every leading professional surfed at Malibu and though he won the final from Buzzy Kerbox, Wayne Bartholomew and Shaun Tomson, Mark's main recollection of the week in California is one of homesickness, poor surf and even poorer accommodation: 'All I could think of was how soon can I go home.'

This was a strange experience for Mark. It was his first trip to Malibu though not his first exposure to the teeming polyglot beach culture of America, so unlike the relatively pristine Australian and north shore beaches where the activities were restricted to surfing and sunbaking. Mark was uncomfortable with the crowds, most of whom weren't

---

[*] The board used by Horan, which was so effective in the minimal surf, was shaped by leading South African craftsman Spider Murphy, who made many of Shaun Tomson's surfboards.

there for the waves, the inaccessibility, and the oppressive policing of activity in and out of the water: 'Beaches in California remind me of a fortress.' Still the selective traveller, Mark only went to Malibu because of the pressure Horan had applied by winning in Brazil. His motel room was dark, airless and very hot. 'I couldn't wait to get out of there. The whole thing was like a zoo.'

The tour then diverted to Japan for an event sponsored by Marui, a department store chain that are still heavily involved in surfing sponsorship, unlike many of the other sponsors of the early 1980s. In the Marui in good surf Mark finished equal third behind winner Bartholomew and in so doing wrested the ratings lead from Horan. Going into his favoured Hawaiian leg Mark was ahead of Horan and looking hard at title number three.

As both Horan and Richards both did poorly in the Pipeline Masters, it rested on the final event, the World Cup, to decide the world title winner. In the first round of the World Cup at Haleiwa, Richards emphatically won his heat to throw down the gauntlet to Horan, who finished fifth in his heat later in the day. Paul Holmes, writing in *Surfer* magazine, described Mark's victory:

> *The whole act, under the available conditions, was flawless. Over the years surfing has seen some great riders but nobody has come even close to this man when it comes to being what a champion sportsman OUGHT to be. His actual surfing is as good, if not better, than any who have gone before, regardless of past limitations in equipment and technology. His wave judgment and selection are uncanny. His strategy and tactics are almost always perfectly suited to the occasion. As a representative of the sport he is beyond reproach . . . Richards is possibly the greatest surfer ever to ride a wave.*

Mark trades tips with Jack Sonni, former Dire Straits guitarist, in Los Angeles in 1987.

Although neither Horan nor Richards reached the final, Richards went two rounds further than Horan and so kept the title from his young challenger. Richards had accomplished his goal of setting records that would be hard to beat but he wanted more. Mark Warren remembers that Mark 'wanted to be remembered as more than a great surfer. He wanted to be a legend.'

Mark Richards is self-deprecating on just about anything except his surfing. About that he is rightfully proud. He can look back not just at his fabulous record, but also at the way he surfed. He developed an expertise that was unmatched by any one of the hundreds of thousands of people who surfed all around the world in Australia, the US, New Zealand, South Africa, the West Indies, England, France, Indonesia, Brazil, Peru. Take away the trophies, the money, the thunderous applause and what are you left with? The best surfer in the world. And for Richards to stand out from his rivals was important. The man who wouldn't volubly promote himself out of the water had unequivocal beliefs about his standing in the sport. To Mark, image and presence were important and he wasn't afraid to go to certain lengths to establish an identity for himself. For much of his career, he has been identified with the MR logo, his initials inside a Superman logo designed for him in 1975 by Hawaiian artist Albert Dove. It's hardly the badge of a shrinking violet: 'I wasn't self-conscious about it then but I am now when I look back at some of the pictures. I had huge ones on the boards and the wetsuits. It is semi-embarrassing. I probably was an ego maniac.'

Mark surfs Hawaii in 1976, the year the professional circuit was born.
PHOTO: BERNIE BAKER"LEONARD BRADY/ISLAND STYLE

CHAPTER SIX

ONCE MORE, WITH FEELING

By the start of 1982, the IPS tour had grown to twelve events in six countries and a total prize pool of more than $350 000. Much of the early ground had been broken and the tour was attracting a swelling band of young hopefuls from Australia, the east and west coasts of the US, Hawaii, Brazil and South Africa. Qualifying trials had enormous fields, were hotly contested and offered prize money of their own. In 1981 Tom Carroll had earned a top 16 seed because of Chris Byrne's early and sad retirement and he made the most of the opportunity by finishing the year ranked ninth. Carroll, Martin Potter and the prodigious Californian Tom Curren, who was to make his professional debut in 1982, were being spoken of as future champions.

But there were also plenty of other newcomers making things difficult for the established seeds. They included Australians Greg Day, Richard Cram, Terry Richardson,

Glen Winton and Gary Timperley, South Africans Marc Price and Mike Savage, American Wes Laine from the eastern State of Virginia and Hawaiians Denton Miyamura, Tony Moniz and Vince Klyn. It was obvious Richards had far more than his usual challengers to worry about if he were going to succeed in winning his fourth world title.

But once more the sternest test would come from Cheyne Horan. By this stage Horan was perceived as one of the world's best small-wave surfers and his competitive strategy had improved hugely. Mark thought the surfing media, in particular, wanted a new hero and detected a strengthening push in certain quarters for Horan to usurp the throne. While Mark revelled in his relative anonymity in Newcastle, the Bondi-based Horan was much more accessible to both the surfing and non-surfing media and he was attracting considerable attention. At times he appeared to have the entourage of a rock star. Judge, contest organiser and now ASP executive director Graham Cassidy says Horan's easygoing, open, friendly nature made him a sitting duck: 'It wasn't his fault that he got all the attention. He was just so personable, so accessible and at Cheyne's it was open house all the time. He's always been a vulnerable, insecure person so maybe he needed all those people around him. But I'm not sure it was a good thing because for a few years there I don't think Cheyne made a decision for himself. Mark was completely the opposite. He came from a tight knit, happy family. He had security. He didn't need anyone else and if people had tried to hang around him he would have told them to go away. The rivalry between Cheyne and Mark went through stages and it got quite bitter for a while, particularly on Cheyne's side. He was really down on Mark and though it wasn't personal I think for a while he let it get to him. Certainly at one stage it got a bit nasty and Mark had a few cryptic comments to make about Cheyne. By 1982 Cheyne was into things like herbalism and generally was presenting an alternative sort of image whereas Mark was so conservative, so much the family man. I think he thought to himself there was no way somebody like Cheyne, who stood for a different lifestyle, was going to take the title from him.'

Horan and Richards clashed in the final of the year's first event, the Straight Talk Tyres Open, in tiny, windblown surf at Elouera Beach near Cronulla. Horan's support from the big and vocal crowd was far greater than that for Richards, who appeared pedestrian in the minute waves compared to the speeding Horan. In a best-of-three final, Horan won 2–0.

The tour then moved on to Burleigh Heads where the two again met in the final. The surf was small but this time it looked as though Richards would reverse the result, until he made a huge tactical blunder and sat outside waiting for a big wave that never came. Horan won by half a point and took his ratings lead and fresh confidence down to Bells Beach. Horan had won his first 12 heats of 1982 before finally losing to Tom Carroll in the quarter-finals at Bells. Carroll reached the final, which he lost to Richards who completed his record fourth Bells victory.

The Surfabout was the last event on the Australian leg of the tour and interest focused on whether Horan could maintain his ratings lead. The year before Horan had won a bizarre heat in Surfabout when he surfed North Narrabeen by himself after arch rival Jim Banks failed to show up until the closing minutes. In round three of the 1982 Surfabout, Banks atoned for his terrible blunder when he beat Horan in poor waves at South Avalon. Mark Richards only went one round further before being stopped by a rampaging Martin

Richards leaves a well-defined trench mark in Burleigh Heads, 1979. PHOTO: PETER CRAWFORD

Richards lacerates big surf in Haleiwa, Hawaii, in the 1979 World Cup final.
PHOTO: BERNIE BAKER-LEONARD BRADY/ISLAND STYLE

High time at Burleigh Heads, Australia: Richards arcs off the top during the Stubbies contest in 1979.
PHOTO: PETER CRAWFORD

Richards tests his injured ankle in Haleiwa, Hawaii, in 1983.
PHOTO: BERNIE BAKER-LEONARD BRADY/ISLAND STYLE

Richards has most of his board out of the water as he turns at Haleiwa, Hawaii, in 1983.
PHOTO: BERNIE BAKER-LEONARD BRADY/ISLAND STYLE

High flier: Richards surfs Bells Beach, Australia in 1985. PHOTO: SURFING WORLD

Potter but it was enough to get the lead back from Horan before the tour left for Bali.[*]

After skipping Indonesia Mark made his third and final trip to South Africa, where he increased his lead over Horan by winning the Gunston 500 from his old rival Wayne Bartholomew. Neither he nor Horan had any impact on the next two events, the Mainstay Magnum in Durban and the Waimea 5000 in Brazil. Mark lost an atrociously conceived heat against Richard Cram in the Mainstay in a re-run of his embarrassing, sit-and-wait episode at Burleigh Heads. Both surfers jockeyed for position for 15 minutes, playing a ridiculous game of cat and mouse and completely ignoring the fact that they had no chance of catching a wave where they were. Mark remembers the announcer saying "'Richard Cram and Mark Richards, you have got to move into the line-up to catch waves. There are no waves where you are sitting." So eventually I thought "Screw this, I can beat this guy. I don't need to play these stupid games" so I just went thrashing past him because I saw a set coming but I missed it by three strokes. I reckon I was three strokes away from winning that heat because as it turned out it was by far and away the best wave, the one I missed. It was another example of my not being fit enough.'

Horan stormed back into contention in the inaugural OP Pro before a jam-packed Huntington Beach. The OP Pro went on to become one of surfing's great tournaments with multiple winners Tom Curren, Mark Occhilupo and Barton

---

[*] Underscoring how professional surfing was expanding was the extraordinary tale of Tony McDonagh in the Surfabout. McDonagh, with no great contest credentials, was well down the alternates' list for the 128-man trials which, happily for him, were held at his home beach of Curl Curl. So McDonagh sat on the sand and hoped there would be enough no-shows for him to get a start. There were, and in an amazing display of tenacity he survived a cutthroat repechage heat to make it into the main event where he drew . . . Mark Richards. Exit Tony McDonagh.

Lynch. Massive crowds blanket the beach right down to the water and line the famous Huntington Beach pier to provide great outdoor theatre. Blond, blue-eyed, handsome Cheyne Horan looked like the all-Californian boy and the 1982 crowd took him to their hearts. When he wasn't signing autographs he was winning heats, including the final against Shaun Tomson. The South African had put Mark out in the semi-finals so before the final Mark stressed to Shaun that he must beat Cheyne to keep him at arm's length in the race for the title: 'But Cheyne virtually had it won from the first or second wave when he did a backhand 360-degree turn right next to the pier on a big wave. The crowd went crazy and Shaun's heart must have sunk. A ride like that must have a big effect on the judges. They are supposed to be unbiased but crowd reaction pushes them over the edge. The judge is considering whether to give a ride like Cheyne's a 9 or a 9.5 and the crowd is going absolutely mad. I think they would be tempted to give it a 9.5. They are influenced by the fact the crowd likes it. It gives a surfer that little extra push. So after Cheyne's ride it was all downhill for Shaun. Cheyne was so on, Shaun could not peg him back no matter what he did.'

Victory put Horan ahead in the ratings with just three events to go. Horan increased his lead by finishing ahead of Richards in Japan's Marui Pro, which was won by 1982 world amateur champion Tom Curren in only his second major professional outing. Earlier he had beaten Tom Carroll in round one of the OP Pro and he repeated the effort in the final of the Marui, as Mark recalls: 'Tom [Carroll] was pulling off straight up and down but Curren was even MORE vertical. He was coming off the bottom and nearly going back around the same track, the full rotation off the top, and in that contest I remember thinking he had uncanny wave judgment and sense. For some reason he always gets the good waves. It has been that way throughout his whole career. Even if someone has him on the ropes with five seconds to go in a heat the gift wave appears and he's off on a winning ride.'

Curren's impact on the professional scene was sudden and dramatic but it was no fluke. For years he had honed his skills in an exhaustive amateur competition program in California and at the world titles in 1980, where he won the juniors, and 1982, where he won the open title but lost the juniors to Australian Bryce Ellis. Like his father Pat, Curren is a reclusive, taciturn man. The most successful American surfer of all time, Tom Curren hindered his marketability by moving to France to live in the late 1980s. In 1990 he made history by becoming the first surfer to regain the world championship, having won it in 1985 and 1986. His feat was all the more magnificent considering he had given up his seeding and had to battle through three rounds of trials to reach the main events. At the end of the 1991 season he led the all-time major contest winners list with 32 from Tom Carroll (25) and Mark Richards (17). His surfing became the yardstick by which all others were measured. Mick Adam, a fine surfer from Merewether and a close friend of Richards for more than 20 years, believes Curren is the only surfer who may be of the same calibre as Richards. 'But I think Mark was the greatest there ever was and possibly ever will be.'

It was now left to the two Hawaiian events, the Pipeline Masters and the World Cup, to decide the 1982 world championship. Mark went to Hawaii meaning business. He shelved his twin fins for the time being, reverting to single fins to tackle the bigger waves. As Pipeline breaks left, Mark, a natural footer, went in search of every left hander he could find. He also took to riding Pipeline more before the first contest to get used to the wave. This notorious reef break is close to the beach and as such is highly photogenic and consequently very crowded. Even if you were the only surfer out on a medium sized day, you would be risking your life at Pipeline, such is the power and trickiness of the wave and the sharpness of the shallow coral reef. It was a chore for Mark to frequent a beach he normally avoided in favour of less intense spots, which were of less interest to the photographers. 'I don't have a good relationship with Pipeline. I would not class myself as a good Pipeline surfer. Frankly, the place scares me. It's not the size of the waves, it's the bottom. I have had one of the worst wipeouts of my life there where I went head first into the bottom. Since that wipeout the day before the 1985 Pipeline Masters, I haven't gone left at Pipeline ever again. That wipeout was a big shock to the system and it put me out of the water for two weeks. I lost interest in it after that because you read all the horror stories and you think those things won't happen to me and when it did I thought I don't need this place that badly. I really think looking back on it I'm very lucky to be here now. The two worst wipeouts I've had in my life are indirectly attributable to my friend Randy Rarick. Once he told me Waimea was worth checking out and I went there and got thrashed, and then this time he told me Pipeline was good and not too crowded. It was more crowded than he said and I had not had a wave for a while so I made the stupid mistake of paddling for one of the last waves of a set on the inside. I just stood up and fell out of the sky and I was going over and over inside it and I remember thinking "I hope I don't hit the bottom" and then next thing, wham! I have never hit anything that hard ever. It was like being hit with a baseball bat in the knee, shoulder and head. I actually thought the side of my head was gone. I just flashed on Beaver [Florida surfer Steve Massefeller, shockingly hurt in a Pipeline wipeout] and I thought I would black out and drown. I got to the surface and was seeing stars and I felt the side of my face and I thought "Great, it's still all there, I am all right". There was blood streaming over my hand. I had concussion but nothing was broken. I drove home and walked in the door and asked Jenny if she could fix this up, showing her my injury. She just about passed out. She drove me to the hospital at Kuhuku. I was bandaged and x-rayed at the hospital. The only thing that saved me was that where I hit was toward the end of the wave and I hit flat reef. If I had hit one of the big sharp bits of coral that stick up at Pipeline it would have gone through my head.' That is apparently what happened to Joaquin Miro 'Shigi' Quesada, a Peruvian surfer who was decapitated at the Pipeline in the 1960s.

Mark left nothing to chance as he prepared for his showdown with Horan in the 1982 Pipeline Masters: 'Pipeline is one of the places you can never count on whereas at Sunset I could be pretty sure I would do OK. But it's the luck of the draw at Pipe and if it's big and fat a natural footer is in with a chance, but if it's hollow and you're up against goofyfooters you are looking at fourth place in your heat.' Horan departed early in the Pipeline Masters while Richards surfed right through to second place behind old rival Michael Ho, who surfed throughout the contest with his broken wrist in a fibreglass cast.

Going into the World Cup Horan had surrendered the world title ratings lead and at Sunset, Richards was unlikely to give it back. He finished second to Tom Carroll in the four-man final, having clinched the world championship by winning his semi-final: 'It was disappointing not to win that final but I had won the world title before the final. Cheyne had been eliminated so I didn't care. It was such a relief to have been on the road all year trying to win the title and then the moment comes when I had won and all other things ceased to matter. I remember sitting on the porch of Bernie Baker's house after the final and Tom was ringing his dad back in Australia, telling him he had just beaten me in the final and I could not care less because I had won the world title.'

The serenity that came with the fourth world title success contrasted starkly with the inner turmoil Mark had felt before the World Cup. Mark had been desperate not to lose his crown. He was number one and wanted to stay there. But his self-confidence had been sapped by the constant pressure the Horan campaign had exerted throughout 1982. Mark was no longer supremely confident he had what it took to keep the youngster at bay. He took the unusual step of seeking advice from 1976 world champion Peter Townend, not a particularly close friend but a man whose determination and focus Mark had always admired. Townend, who wasn't a contender for the title, assured Mark there was nothing wrong with his surfing and that he could still finish at the top of the heap. Mark felt this pep talk had definitely helped him in his preparation for the title-deciding World Cup.

The previous two presentations for the world title had been low key, just like the first one in 1979, but in 1982, IPS went up-market and held the awards ceremony in a function at what was then the Kuilima Hotel, now called the Turtle Bay Hilton. Once again there was no cash, no bonus, not even a watch. The sum total of Mark's prize was a replica wooden car fashioned because of an earlier chance remark by Mark about the amount of trophies making it difficult for him to fit his car in the garage. After the presentation Mark went home for Christmas in Newcastle. 'Bill Delaney was making the update of *Free Ride* and he wanted me to stay to get some footage and I just said "Bill, I'm out of here. I have not been home since 1976 for Christmas and New Year".'

Early in 1983 Mark Richards decided his world championship days were over. He had had enough. By now his back was causing him enormous trouble and the pressure of being on top for so long had taken its toll: 'It was a conscious decision. It was probably during 1981 and 1982 that my back really started worrying me and I was always worried my back would go out before a contest and I wouldn't be able to start. Besides, I had completely lost the desire and the mental application to go on. I honestly do not think I could have gone on and done another tour even if I had wanted to. I had had enough. It had been four years, two years full on. I had been living with the pressure of "Cheyne's going to do it this year, Cheyne will finally get him". Virtually I felt it was like me against everyone, as though the pendulum had swung where everyone is cheering for Cheyne and I just thought "That's it".'

As it turned out Mark Richards would never have been a player in the 1983 title race, which was to extend through to April 1984 under the ASP's new, non-calendar year season. He was hit by a huge wave at Dixon Park and tore ankle ligaments, which kept him out of the water for five frustrating months. Earlier he had demonstrated in tiny, unsuitable left handers at North Narrabeen that he was still competitive by reaching the semi-finals of Surfabout before losing to eventual final winner Tom Carroll. Prophetically, three of the four Australian events in 1983 were won by Carroll, Tom Curren and Martin Potter. Mark Richards would not win again until his back-to-back Billabong victories in 1985 and 1986. Horan would win again in 1984,

At Stradbroke Island, Queensland, in the mid-1980s: to Mark Richards, surfing has always been about fun.
PHOTO: SURFING WORLD

1985 and remarkably in 1989 at Sunset Beach, but the world title would elude him as Carroll, Curren, Potter, Mark Occhilupo, Gary Elkerton, Damien Hardman and Barton Lynch became the superstars of the professional circuit, supplanting Richards, Horan, Bartholomew, Kealoha and Tomson.

Richards continued to compete sporadically, which may have been a mistake: 'I had no passion, no fire, like I had had in the world championship years. I was just there making up the numbers. I did not really want to stop but the smart thing would have been to walk away. I still enjoyed the lifestyle. I had been a touring professional for almost 10 years to varying degrees so to just stop and stay at home after all that time would have been very difficult. I didn't want to compete full-on but I still wanted to travel and the only avenue for travel that I could see was surfing competition. During this time I was dropping heats to people that two or three years earlier would have been unthinkable. I was not winning anything but I was having a good time and that's why I kept going. It was relaxing and there was absolutely no pressure and just by turning up at contests I was keeping my sponsors happy. I was not going to bed at night thinking ratings points or worrying whether Cheyne would beat me. If I lost a heat I just shrugged.'

Facing up to the Hawaiian surf in 1976.
PHOTO: BERNIE BAKER- LEONARD BRADY/ISLAND STYLE

CHAPTER SEVEN

'I FEEL FOR HIM'

The Horan/Richards rivalry was pro surfing's great sideshow of the early 1980s. Horan, three-and-a-half years younger than Richards, appeared at first almost a fabricated stereotype of an Australian surf youngster. He was short and compact, blue-eyed and baby-faced, with a mop of blond hair. And he was from Bondi, the quintessential Australian beach.

Horan's appearance, background and extraordinary talent attracted a plethora of silly cliches and tags. He had finished second to Wayne Bartholomew in the 1978 world title race and the following year went within a heat of the title, only to watch it go to Mark Richards on an amazing day at Haleiwa in Hawaii. He slipped back to fifth in 1980 as Richards dominated the year but bounced back to be a close second in 1981 and 1982. At one point in the 1982 contest at Sunset Beach, Mark Richards thought he had given Cheyne Horan the opportunity to get past him and finally win his first world title. Richards was shattered: 'I just about cried,' he says. 'All I could think of was I was out and he was in and it landed on me like a ton of bricks.' Richards did in fact clinch the world title but he says that moment of total desolation gave him insight into what it must have been like for Cheyne Horan to finish second, four times. A world title, once considered foregone for Horan, never eventuated. In 1992 he embarked on his 16th consecutive world tour, ranked 30th, still apparently with fire in his belly and still one of the fittest surfers on tour.

In his teens, Horan appeared to be the epitome of the eat-sleep-and-drink surf animal. However, as he grew older the peripatetic Horan became an unconventional and at times controversial figure, embracing unorthodox views on things such as lifestyle and surfboard design. He has strong opinions on issues such as pollution control and world peace.

Horan is a tough, uncompromising competitor with plenty of determination. Saddled when he was young with a reputation of being inadequate in big waves, Horan worked hard on that part of his surfing to develop into one of the sport's more daring and accomplished big-wave riders. A high point of the enigmatic Horan's career came in December 1989 when he easily won the Billabong Pro at Sunset Beach to join an elite few who have won contests in Hawaii and to accomplish the even rarer feat of winning back a place in the top 16 rankings.

Of their well publicised rivalry, Mark Richards says: 'Cheyne was pretty much my main rival in the years when I was trying to win the world title. There were a lot of guys who were hard to beat as well but Cheyne was the main one and I think everyone credits me with ruining Cheyne's life by the fact that he did not win a world title. But what they forget is that I only beat him three times and that it was Rabbit [Bartholomew] who beat him the other time. We have never been enemies but we have never been the best of friends either. We always said "Hello" and talked to each other but it is really hard to be friendly with someone you are competing against all the time, someone who could be standing in your way of winning a world title. It is an interesting relationship you have with them. You kind of wish a lot of the time they did not exist.

'But the fact that he came so close never came up for discussion between us. He has never said anything to me and I've never said anything to him about it but, strangely enough, I do not feel guilty about it but I do think about it at times. It made me stop and think in 1982 when I thought he might have won. I have often wondered how I would have coped if it had been me coming second. It would have been so hard to live with and deal with had the shoe been on the other foot. I feel for him.

'There was probably no-one more stoked for him than I was when he won the Billabong. It was the biggest and most desirable event to win at that stage and the $US50 000 first prize made me so happy for him. I had an ear to ear grin when I found out.'

A nimble surfer with a low centre of gravity and the light-footed agility to skip over the top of small, slow waves, Horan seldom conformed to general opinion when it came to surfboard design. In 1983 Horan shunned the increasingly-popular, three-fin boards, electing instead to fit the winged keel the late Ben Lexcen had designed for the 1983 America's Cup 12-metre yacht challenge. Winged keels on surfboards did not become popular whereas Simon Anderson's three-fin idea became universal. As Mark comments: 'Cheyne was a phenomenal, terrific surfer. I

Richards's classic bottom turn: it's easy after you've done thousands. This one is at Merewether Beach, Australia, in 1985. PHOTO: SURFING WORLD

Richards surfs Pinballs at Waimea Bay, Hawaii, in 1985.
PHOTO: BERNIE BAKER-LEONARD BRADY/ISLAND STYLE

Mark's backhand surfing was always strong, as he demonstrates in Hawaii.
PHOTO: BERNIE BAKER-LEONARD BRADY/ISLAND STYLE

Cheyne Horan gets radical on conventional equipment. The Richards/Horan rivalry was the greatest battle in pro surfing during the early 1980s. PHOTO: MARTIN TULLEMANS

think his undoing was that he was a bit of a crusader in terms of board design. He was too experimental in the types of boards he was using in competition, particularly in Hawaii. I thought he was sabotaging himself a lot of the time. He actually made it easier for me because I knew the boards that he had were so left field, even before the winged keel days, that they were not going to work in big surf. It's ironic how well he does in big waves now. In 1981 and 1982 when the lead used to see-saw and the tour finished in Hawaii I always felt confident as long as I was in striking distance going into Hawaii. I knew I could peg him back in Hawaii because I had a much better track record there competitively and I always thought I could surf bigger waves better than him. I guess he was more timid in those days. He has done a complete 360 from not being acknowledged as a big-wave surfer, his weak point, to it now being one of his strongest points.'

Cheyne Horan does not believe Mark Richards should have won four world titles. Two, yes, but not four. Horan feels the other two were rightfully his. The reason, he says, was that Richards was the benefactor of favourable decisions from Lightning Bolt representatives on the judging panel: 'Mark had a big following because he was sponsored by Lightning Bolt. At the time he had a lot of push and I perceived a big bias towards him. If he had not had that Lightning Bolt support then no way would he have won four world titles. There were heats I should have won where I would get a 3–2 decision against me. I got doused out of a couple of heats I should have won. I'd say really he won two world titles and I won two. Thankfully now the rules have changed and you can't have your sponsors judging you.'

Unsurprisingly, Richards takes issue with Horan's recollection: 'Cheyne seems to be forgetting that Wayne

Bartholomew won the world title one of the four times he was runner-up. I won the 1980 title by what I think is still a record margin so I think the only two titles in question are in 1981 and 1982. As for the so-called Lightning Bolt conspiracy I preferred not to have those people judging me because there were times I was on the losing end of a 3–2 decision as they over-compensated trying not to be biased. I won my world titles fair and square. Again, I must say what militated against Cheyne was his crusading attitude toward new equipment and his lack of experience in Hawaii.'

Horan thinks that if he had actually won the world title it's highly probable he would have followed Richards into retirement. 'But I'm OK. I'm still surfing, I'm still competing, I've still got my health. Perhaps I'll write a book when I retire at 40 after I have set more records.' Horan says he never really knew Richards, having almost no contact with him away from contests, but he acknowledges the part the champion played in his life: 'He really had good standards. His preparation for contests was really good. He was always ready. Like, if it was raining MR would have a raincoat for when he was waiting for his heat or if it was sunny he would have found some shade to sit in. And he's always been an upright sort of person, though we didn't know each other away from contests. He influenced my life, he had a huge impact. He showed me what could be done. He and his father had a giant influence over me. It seemed like his Dad ran him like a racehorse. Ray knew when to give him space and then at other times he would be all over MR, telling him what to do. I had my support, Geoff McCoy and Paul Neilsen, and MR had his father. I look back and I realise I was up against a good team.'

The other surfers who rivalled Mark Richards for his world titles were Wayne Bartholomew and Shaun Tomson.

Following a tradition of great Gold Coast power surfers such as Peter Drouyn, Paul Neilsen and Michael Peterson, Bartholomew was brash, outspoken and hugely ambitious. He contested every heat with an intensity that many rivals found discomfiting.

'We had some great heats,' says Mark of the 1978 world champion. 'Wayne was probably one of the hardest people to surf against because he was a thinker. When heats became man on man* it became more of a strategic battle against the other person rather than in the old days of the four and six-man heats when you simply tried to keep to yourself and hoped the waves would come through. So as well as surfing well you had to really out-think and out-position him for the sets to get the good rides. Rabbit was a great strategist who had a real presence in the water. I think Rabbit found it pretty easy to psyche people out because he was so up and ready all the time. You went into a heat with Bugs and you knew he wasn't tentatively thinking "Can I beat this guy?" He just knew he could win. After all it was rare that someone beat him. So during the years I was competing he was one of my toughest rivals because he always surfed really well and he always planned really well. And if the waves were hollow it was even worse because he was a great tube rider. It's the same these days. The surfer who manages to get a few tube rides usually will win the heat.

'And of course he was a great hustler for position. He was one of those people you could never take the inside

---

* Until the 1977 Stubbies Classic at Burleigh Heads in Queensland most contests, amateur and professional, were run with a minimum of four-contestant heats. For the old Makaha contests in Hawaii as many as fifteen competitors would take to the water at the same time. Peter Drouyn, the 1970 Australian champion, was one of Australia's most successful surfers of all time and one of the sport's more outspoken and flamboyant characters. Drouyn had the idea of putting just two surfers in the water at the same time. It would be less cluttered, the result would be more clear cut and the emphasis would be more on surfing than luck. Two-man heats revolutionised contest surfing.

position from but you knew he had a very good chance of getting it from you. There was no priority buoy in those days so you had to stay alert to keep the inside spot. I am sure that Rabbit, with his intensity, his savvy and his burning will to win intimidated quite a few guys.'

Richards had competed against Bartholomew since the amateur days in the early 1970s so perhaps some of the mind games rubbed off on him. Short of violence, Richards tried to make things as unpleasant as possible for his rivals. 'It's hard to describe but it was just your presence in the water, particularly if you were up against a young guy,' he says. 'You never left someone alone, never left them unmolested in the water. You would always be on their case, paddling beside them and paddling inside them, trying to get the inside spot. If a wave came through you would do everything you could to dispute who had the right to take off. It was a bit like the bully in the school yard. There was no priority system as they have in pro contests now. You paddle around the priority buoy and you have the unchallengeable right to whatever comes through. In those days it was so different to the way it is now. It must be very hard for the superstars of today, such as Damien Hardman, Tom Carroll, Tom Curren and Barton Lynch, to apply that sort of bullying pressure the way we did. It's all because of this turn system. Even if a less experienced surfer was competing against one of the more aggressive surfers they would know that when it's their turn there's nothing the other guy can do about it. I think if it had been the way it is now I may have won more contests. I know you should never say "if this" or "if that" but I truly believe the current system would have favoured me. I felt my surfing was my strong point and though my hustling ability was pretty good it wasn't as good as some of the other guys. Realistically, the turn system is probably a fairer assessment of ability. I have seen so many heats decided because one guy was prevented from catching a wave. I saw Cheyne lose a heat in Japan during one of my world title years because Buzzy Kerbox did not let him ride a wave. Buzzy got every wave that came through and managed to apply so much pressure on Cheyne he didn't catch anything to score on. Yet there was no question that Cheyne was a better surfer than Buzzy.'

Horan was no mean hassler himself but he was well and truly on the receiving end of a lesson in the ignoble art from Peter Townend in a semi-final of the 1979 World Cup, the final event of the year. Townend kept Horan at bay with expert paddling and positioning to win the heat that would have clinched a world title for the youngster from Bondi. Richards then beat Townend in the final and a dynasty began. Richards still rates Townend, Paul Neilsen and Hawaiian Michael Ho as the cleverest hustlers he has encountered in competition.

Having acknowledged that professional surfing's current system, which places a heavier emphasis on wave-riding skills, is probably a fairer way of achieving a result Richards recalls the more primitive days with affection. 'I really think that strategy and gamesmanship are big parts of surfing and I think contests lack something without them. Really, most competitive sport is just an extension of recreational sport. When you go surfing at your local beach there are no priority buoys. Positioning, the ability to be in the right place at the right time, is what gets you the wave and there should always be an element of that in competition.'

After his extraordinary three-victory burst late in 1975 and early 1976, Mark Richards was hailed as the hottest surfer in the world. But the youngster then embarked on an important phase in his quest for knowledge of what makes a surfboard work and he went for two years without a victory as he developed and refined his twin-fin theories. During this time Shaun Tomson, a South African surfer, quickly established a reputation for being one of the most innovative and perhaps the best surfer in the world. Tall and handsome, Shaun was the son of Ernie Tomson, a champion surf swimmer from Durban who believed wholeheartedly in his son's future as a surfer. Shaun had begun surfing in 1965, in the longboard era, and gained international recognition four years later when he appeared surfing Jeffreys Bay in the late Bob Evans' film *The Way We Like It*. In 1970 he was the youngest competitor at the world titles in Victoria. Mark Richards believes that Shaun Thomson is the greatest tube rider ever. 'He really changed the way people rode in the barrel. It was not until Shaun came along that people started thinking there are different ways to go through a barrel other than just in a straight line. The main thing he did was to manoeuvre inside the tube and follow the contour of the tube as it would twist or bend, get bigger or smaller. He was adapting to whatever the wave did and he had that wide stance that was really perfect for the way he surfed. He was turning a little bit with his front foot. It was like his front foot and his arm were guiding him through the tube. An absolutely incredible surfer, best tube rider ever. And the other thing about Shaun was that he was one of surfing's great ambassadors at a time when we really needed such people. He was a most articulate and intelligent spokesman for the sport.'

A tally of the individual successes of the Richards, Horan, Bartholomew and Thomson line-up shows that Horan has had eleven tour victories and season finishes of 29, 2, 2, 5, 2, 2, 3, 5, 15, 17, 24, 19, 14, 17, 30 from 1977 until

1991. In twelve man-on-man clashes with Richards, Horan won seven to Richards' five.

Bartholomew had eight tour victories and finished 27, 2, 1, 3, 4, 4, 5, 2, 15, 24, 30 from 1976 to 1986. In eleven man-on-man clashes, Richards won eight to Bartholomew's three.

Tomson had twelve tour victories and finished 6, 1, 4, 6, 3, 5, 4, 6, 2, 12, 9, 11, 13, 20 from 1976 until 1989. Tomson won all six of his man-on-man heats with Mark Richards.

CHAPTER EIGHT

TRAGEDY,
KING AND
THAT BACK

Back pain had been distressing Mark Richards more and more since he first experienced it as a teenager in the 1970s. It eventually had a huge impact on his life and his surfing. But it was slight compared with the agony he and his wife Jenny would have to endure. In late 1989 their second son, Beau, died from Sudden Infant Death Syndrome, the sinister and baffling cot death. Beau was two months old. Mark and Jenny were devastated.

Six months before Beau died Mark's closest friend, his father Ray died from a heart attack at the age of seventy-one. When an earthquake visited death and destruction on Newcastle on 27 December, 1989, its consequences, including extensive damage to the surf shop Ray and Val had worked so hard to establish, were largely lost on already numbed Mark and Jenny Richards. As Mark explains, 'Losing a child is something you can never be prepared for. You can come to terms with the fact your parents will probably die before you. But you just never think your children will die before you.' Heartbreak like this was not supposed to happen to Mark and Jenny Richards, the wonderful, popular young couple with so much going for them. Richards had faced tough challenges in his life but nothing like this. As he was still trying to come to terms with the death of his father, the man he called King, he then had to deal with a tragedy beyond comprehension and work to steer his family through the pain. As expected he showed great courage, a courage more than matched by his loving partner, Jenny.

Mark Richards met Jenny Jobson in August, 1976, on a blind date at the Beach Hotel, a popular spot that overlooks his favourite surfing break and which is a haunt of the members of Merewether Surfboard Club. Jenny Jobson was no bleached beach bunny. Dark of hair and eye and pale of skin, she was a bright, lively, humorous girl in her first year of teachers college in Newcastle. She was sharing a flat with friends, having moved away from her family's home at Pearl Beach on the Central Coast, to the south of Newcastle. Not a proficient swimmer she nonetheless had several friends who surfed and she was a frequent beach goer. She had heard of this surfer called Mark Richards and had told his schoolfriend Neil Slater she wasn't interested in meeting him because she was sure he would be full of self-importance. And she didn't need a blind date, anyhow, thanks very much. But Slater has impressive powers of persuasion and deception and he part-cajoled and part-lured Jenny to the Beach Hotel on the promise she would meet somebody else altogether: 'I was there feeling very nervous and apprehensive, thinking I hope he doesn't come. I can remember saying to Neil he is not going to turn up so I can go home now. But Mark had actually cruised into the bar and was over with some friends and checked me out. He thought if she is no good I can get out of it. He came over with a guy called Glen, who I had thought was the one I was supposed to meet, but he soon disappeared and I put two and two together and realised Mark was my blind date. I hadn't known what he looked like, I just knew him by name. We could not talk very much at the hotel because the music was loud so we just yelled a few words at each other and at closing time at 10 o'clock Neil announced Mark would drive me home. I was a little bit wary but I had little choice because my flat was so far away. Anyhow, I walked out to go home with Mark and there was this panel van and I thought "Oh, no, what have I got myself into?" But he was the perfect gentleman and he drove me home and we sat in the van outside my flat and talked for hours. We got on really well right from the start.'

Jenny's teaching career and Mark's frequent travelling kept them apart more than they would have liked. Jenny recalls how after an uncertain start when they seldom saw each other their relationship flourished: 'In 1979 I finished college and was sent back to the Central Coast and I just used to see Mark on weekends. We were serious and knew we would eventually get married but we were not in any hurry. I had spent all those years studying and wanted to teach and was not prepared to give it up and run around the world with him and be a surfing widow. When we first met I did not really think about what he did. He was not terribly famous, only well-known in Newcastle. I was there as his career developed. It was a gradual thing. I didn't worry about whether he could support us if we got married. I think when you are young and in love you don't worry about things like that. And besides, I was a teacher and had a good income so financial matters didn't worry me. It was fun when I did go places with him. He was so different to my friends' boyfriends who were accountants or mechanics or teachers and they led mundane lives and here we were tripping around the world. Although, it was never as exciting when you got there as you thought it would be because you never got to see any of the country. But it still was fun and with him being a bit of a hero you were treated well and it was exciting to sit back and watch.'

Jenny is neither an apologist nor a detractor of Mark. A recurring impression about this man is that from this youth his close friends have been people who have appreciated his great skill but have also liked him simply for who he is. Their friendship has not been influenced by his stardom. Mick Adam, a friend of more than 20 years from Merewether, says, 'He should have had the biggest head on the planet but he never has. That's very much down to the influence of his parents I would say. The boys at Merewether would have slapped him down if he had got out of line but, no, his home life is the main reason he has turned out the way he is.' Robbie Wood echoes these feelings: 'To me his great quality is that he's such a genuine person. He has great integrity. And he's had the help of a good woman.'

Mark and Jenny married in 1985 and after one pregnancy ended tragically, a beautiful, blond, blue-eyed boy they named Kyle was born in October 1987. For Jenny and Mark, Kyle's birth was very special. Before his arrival Jenny had had a birth induced at 20 weeks because her first baby suffered from a condition called anencephaly, in which the brain does not develop and the child has no chance of survival. The baby, whom they called Elliot and whose tiny

The wedding day: Mark and Jenny in 1985. PHOTO: NEWS LIMITED

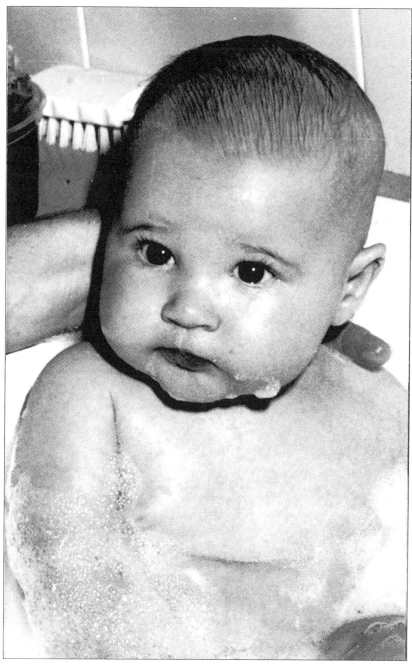

Mark and Jenny's daughter Grace, born in November 1991.
PHOTO: STEFAN MOORE—SUN-HERALD

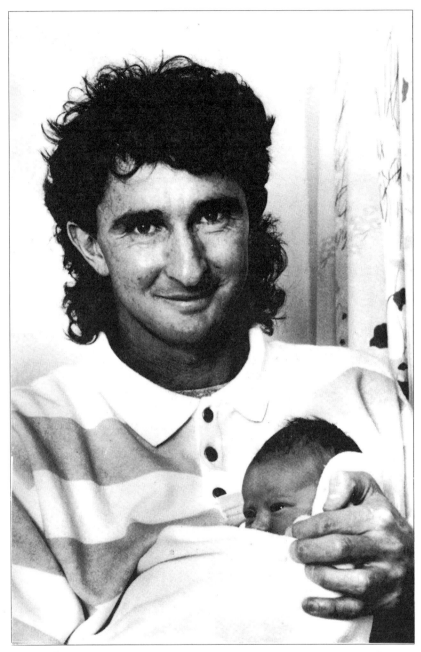

Mark with his son Kyle: 'When Kyle was born it was pretty special.'

Richards tests his injured ankle in Haleiwa, Hawaii, in 1983.
PHOTO: BERNIE BAKER-LEONARD BRADY/ISLAND STYLE

Richards has most of his board out of the water as he turns at Haleiwa, Hawaii, in 1983.
PHOTO: BERNIE BAKER-LEONARD BRADY/ISLAND STYLE

High flier: Richards surfs Bells Beach, Australia in 1985. PHOTO: SURFING WORLD

Potter but it was enough to get the lead back from Horan before the tour left for Bali.[*]

After skipping Indonesia Mark made his third and final trip to South Africa, where he increased his lead over Horan by winning the Gunston 500 from his old rival Wayne Bartholomew. Neither he nor Horan had any impact on the next two events, the Mainstay Magnum in Durban and the Waimea 5000 in Brazil. Mark lost an atrociously conceived heat against Richard Cram in the Mainstay in a re-run of his embarrassing, sit-and-wait episode at Burleigh Heads. Both surfers jockeyed for position for 15 minutes, playing a ridiculous game of cat and mouse and completely ignoring the fact that they had no chance of catching a wave where they were. Mark remembers the announcer saying "'Richard Cram and Mark Richards, you have got to move into the line-up to catch waves. There are no waves where you are sitting." So eventually I thought "Screw this, I can beat this guy. I don't need to play these stupid games" so I just went thrashing past him because I saw a set coming but I missed it by three strokes. I reckon I was three strokes away from winning that heat because as it turned out it was by far and away the best wave, the one I missed. It was another example of my not being fit enough.'

Horan stormed back into contention in the inaugural OP Pro before a jam-packed Huntington Beach. The OP Pro went on to become one of surfing's great tournaments with multiple winners Tom Curren, Mark Occhilupo and Barton

---

[*] Underscoring how professional surfing was expanding was the extraordinary tale of Tony McDonagh in the Surfabout. McDonagh, with no great contest credentials, was well down the alternates' list for the 128-man trials which, happily for him, were held at his home beach of Curl Curl. So McDonagh sat on the sand and hoped there would be enough no-shows for him to get a start. There were, and in an amazing display of tenacity he survived a cutthroat repechage heat to make it into the main event where he drew . . . Mark Richards. Exit Tony McDonagh.

Lynch. Massive crowds blanket the beach right down to the water and line the famous Huntington Beach pier to provide great outdoor theatre. Blond, blue-eyed, handsome Cheyne Horan looked like the all-Californian boy and the 1982 crowd took him to their hearts. When he wasn't signing autographs he was winning heats, including the final against Shaun Tomson. The South African had put Mark out in the semi-finals so before the final Mark stressed to Shaun that he must beat Cheyne to keep him at arm's length in the race for the title: 'But Cheyne virtually had it won from the first or second wave when he did a backhand 360-degree turn right next to the pier on a big wave. The crowd went crazy and Shaun's heart must have sunk. A ride like that must have a big effect on the judges. They are supposed to be unbiased but crowd reaction pushes them over the edge. The judge is considering whether to give a ride like Cheyne's a 9 or a 9.5 and the crowd is going absolutely mad. I think they would be tempted to give it a 9.5. They are influenced by the fact the crowd likes it. It gives a surfer that little extra push. So after Cheyne's ride it was all downhill for Shaun. Cheyne was so on, Shaun could not peg him back no matter what he did.'

Victory put Horan ahead in the ratings with just three events to go. Horan increased his lead by finishing ahead of Richards in Japan's Marui Pro, which was won by 1982 world amateur champion Tom Curren in only his second major professional outing. Earlier he had beaten Tom Carroll in round one of the OP Pro and he repeated the effort in the final of the Marui, as Mark recalls: 'Tom [Carroll] was pulling off straight up and down but Curren was even MORE vertical. He was coming off the bottom and nearly going back around the same track, the full rotation off the top, and in that contest I remember thinking he had uncanny wave judgment and sense. For some reason he always gets the good waves. It has been that way throughout his whole career. Even if someone has him on the ropes with five seconds to go in a heat the gift wave appears and he's off on a winning ride.'

Curren's impact on the professional scene was sudden and dramatic but it was no fluke. For years he had honed his skills in an exhaustive amateur competition program in California and at the world titles in 1980, where he won the juniors, and 1982, where he won the open title but lost the juniors to Australian Bryce Ellis. Like his father Pat, Curren is a reclusive, taciturn man. The most successful American surfer of all time, Tom Curren hindered his marketability by moving to France to live in the late 1980s. In 1990 he made history by becoming the first surfer to regain the world championship, having won it in 1985 and 1986. His feat was all the more magnificent considering he had given up his seeding and had to battle through three rounds of trials to reach the main events. At the end of the 1991 season he led the all-time major contest winners list with 32 from Tom Carroll (25) and Mark Richards (17). His surfing became the yardstick by which all others were measured. Mick Adam, a fine surfer from Merewether and a close friend of Richards for more than 20 years, believes Curren is the only surfer who may be of the same calibre as Richards. 'But I think Mark was the greatest there ever was and possibly ever will be.'

It was now left to the two Hawaiian events, the Pipeline Masters and the World Cup, to decide the 1982 world championship. Mark went to Hawaii meaning business. He shelved his twin fins for the time being, reverting to single fins to tackle the bigger waves. As Pipeline breaks left, Mark, a natural footer, went in search of every left hander he could find. He also took to riding Pipeline more before the first contest to get used to the wave. This notorious reef break is close to the beach and as such is highly photogenic and consequently very crowded. Even if you were the only surfer out on a medium sized day, you would be risking your life at Pipeline, such is the power and trickiness of the wave and the sharpness of the shallow coral reef. It was a chore for Mark to frequent a beach he normally avoided in favour of less intense spots, which were of less interest to the photographers. 'I don't have a good relationship with Pipeline. I would not class myself as a good Pipeline surfer. Frankly, the place scares me. It's not the size of the waves, it's the bottom. I have had one of the worst wipeouts of my life there where I went head first into the bottom. Since that wipeout the day before the 1985 Pipeline Masters, I haven't gone left at Pipeline ever again. That wipeout was a big shock to the system and it put me out of the water for two weeks. I lost interest in it after that because you read all the horror stories and you think those things won't happen to me and when it did I thought I don't need this place that badly. I really think looking back on it I'm very lucky to be here now. The two worst wipeouts I've had in my life are indirectly attributable to my friend Randy Rarick. Once he told me Waimea was worth checking out and I went there and got thrashed, and then this time he told me Pipeline was good and not too crowded. It was more crowded than he said and I had not had a wave for a while so I made the stupid mistake of paddling for one of the last waves of a set on the inside. I just stood up and fell out of the sky and I was going over and over inside it and I remember thinking "I hope I don't hit the bottom" and then next thing, wham! I have never hit anything that hard ever. It was like being hit with a baseball bat in the knee, shoulder and head. I actually thought the side of my head was gone. I just flashed on Beaver [Florida surfer Steve Massefeller, shockingly hurt in a Pipeline wipeout] and I thought I would black out and drown. I got to the surface and was seeing stars and I felt the side of my face and I thought "Great, it's still all there, I am all right". There was blood streaming over my hand. I had concussion but nothing was broken. I drove home and walked in the door and asked Jenny if she could fix this up, showing her my injury. She just about passed out. She drove me to the hospital at Kuhuku. I was bandaged and x-rayed at the hospital. The only thing that saved me was that where I hit was toward the end of the wave and I hit flat reef. If I had hit one of the big sharp bits of coral that stick up at Pipeline it would have gone through my head.' That is apparently what happened to Joaquin Miro 'Shigi' Quesada, a Peruvian surfer who was decapitated at the Pipeline in the 1960s.

Mark left nothing to chance as he prepared for his showdown with Horan in the 1982 Pipeline Masters: 'Pipeline is one of the places you can never count on whereas at Sunset I could be pretty sure I would do OK. But it's the luck of the draw at Pipe and if it's big and fat a natural footer is in with a chance, but if it's hollow and you're up against goofyfooters you are looking at fourth place in your heat.' Horan departed early in the Pipeline Masters while Richards surfed right through to second place behind old rival Michael Ho, who surfed throughout the contest with his broken wrist in a fibreglass cast.

Going into the World Cup Horan had surrendered the world title ratings lead and at Sunset, Richards was unlikely to give it back. He finished second to Tom Carroll in the four-man final, having clinched the world championship by winning his semi-final: 'It was disappointing not to win that final but I had won the world title before the final. Cheyne had been eliminated so I didn't care. It was such a relief to have been on the road all year trying to win the title and then the moment comes when I had won and all other things ceased to matter. I remember sitting on the porch of Bernie Baker's house after the final and Tom was ringing his dad back in Australia, telling him he had just beaten me in the final and I could not care less because I had won the world title.'

The serenity that came with the fourth world title success contrasted starkly with the inner turmoil Mark had felt before the World Cup. Mark had been desperate not to lose his crown. He was number one and wanted to stay there. But his self-confidence had been sapped by the constant pressure the Horan campaign had exerted throughout 1982. Mark was no longer supremely confident he had what it took to keep the youngster at bay. He took the unusual step of seeking advice from 1976 world champion Peter Townend, not a particularly close friend but a man whose determination and focus Mark had always admired. Townend, who wasn't a contender for the title, assured Mark there was nothing wrong with his surfing and that he could still finish at the top of the heap. Mark felt this pep talk had definitely helped him in his preparation for the title-deciding World Cup.

The previous two presentations for the world title had been low key, just like the first one in 1979, but in 1982, IPS went up-market and held the awards ceremony in a function at what was then the Kuilima Hotel, now called the Turtle Bay Hilton. Once again there was no cash, no bonus, not even a watch. The sum total of Mark's prize was a replica wooden car fashioned because of an earlier chance remark by Mark about the amount of trophies making it difficult for him to fit his car in the garage. After the presentation Mark went home for Christmas in Newcastle. 'Bill Delaney was making the update of *Free Ride* and he wanted me to stay to get some footage and I just said "Bill, I'm out of here. I have not been home since 1976 for Christmas and New Year".'

Early in 1983 Mark Richards decided his world championship days were over. He had had enough. By now his back was causing him enormous trouble and the pressure of being on top for so long had taken its toll: 'It was a conscious decision. It was probably during 1981 and 1982 that my back really started worrying me and I was always worried my back would go out before a contest and I wouldn't be able to start. Besides, I had completely lost the desire and the mental application to go on. I honestly do not think I could have gone on and done another tour even if I had wanted to. I had had enough. It had been four years, two years full on. I had been living with the pressure of "Cheyne's going to do it this year, Cheyne will finally get him". Virtually I felt it was like me against everyone, as though the pendulum had swung where everyone is cheering for Cheyne and I just thought "That's it".'

As it turned out Mark Richards would never have been a player in the 1983 title race, which was to extend through to April 1984 under the ASP's new, non-calendar year season. He was hit by a huge wave at Dixon Park and tore ankle ligaments, which kept him out of the water for five frustrating months. Earlier he had demonstrated in tiny, unsuitable left handers at North Narrabeen that he was still competitive by reaching the semi-finals of Surfabout before losing to eventual final winner Tom Carroll. Prophetically, three of the four Australian events in 1983 were won by Carroll, Tom Curren and Martin Potter. Mark Richards would not win again until his back-to-back Billabong victories in 1985 and 1986. Horan would win again in 1984,

At Stradbroke Island, Queensland, in the mid-1980s: to Mark Richards, surfing has always been about fun.
PHOTO: SURFING WORLD

1985 and remarkably in 1989 at Sunset Beach, but the world title would elude him as Carroll, Curren, Potter, Mark Occhilupo, Gary Elkerton, Damien Hardman and Barton Lynch became the superstars of the professional circuit, supplanting Richards, Horan, Bartholomew, Kealoha and Tomson.

Richards continued to compete sporadically, which may have been a mistake: 'I had no passion, no fire, like I had had in the world championship years. I was just there making up the numbers. I did not really want to stop but the smart thing would have been to walk away. I still enjoyed the lifestyle. I had been a touring professional for almost 10 years to varying degrees so to just stop and stay at home after all that time would have been very difficult. I didn't want to compete full-on but I still wanted to travel and the only avenue for travel that I could see was surfing competition. During this time I was dropping heats to people that two or three years earlier would have been unthinkable. I was not winning anything but I was having a good time and that's why I kept going. It was relaxing and there was absolutely no pressure and just by turning up at contests I was keeping my sponsors happy. I was not going to bed at night thinking ratings points or worrying whether Cheyne would beat me. If I lost a heat I just shrugged.'

Facing up to the Hawaiian surf in 1976.
PHOTO: BERNIE BAKER- LEONARD BRADY/ISLAND STYLE

CHAPTER SEVEN

'I FEEL FOR HIM'

The Horan/Richards rivalry was pro surfing's great sideshow of the early 1980s. Horan, three-and-a-half years younger than Richards, appeared at first almost a fabricated stereotype of an Australian surf youngster. He was short and compact, blue-eyed and baby-faced, with a mop of blond hair. And he was from Bondi, the quintessential Australian beach.

Horan's appearance, background and extraordinary talent attracted a plethora of silly cliches and tags. He had finished second to Wayne Bartholomew in the 1978 world title race and the following year went within a heat of the title, only to watch it go to Mark Richards on an amazing day at Haleiwa in Hawaii. He slipped back to fifth in 1980 as Richards dominated the year but bounced back to be a close second in 1981 and 1982. At one point in the 1982 contest at Sunset Beach, Mark Richards thought he had given Cheyne Horan the opportunity to get past him and finally win his first world title. Richards was shattered: 'I just about cried,' he says. 'All I could think of was I was out and he was in and it landed on me like a ton of bricks.' Richards did in fact clinch the world title but he says that moment of total desolation gave him insight into what it must have been like for Cheyne Horan to finish second, four times. A world title, once considered foregone for Horan, never eventuated. In 1992 he embarked on his 16th consecutive world tour, ranked 30th, still apparently with fire in his belly and still one of the fittest surfers on tour.

In his teens, Horan appeared to be the epitome of the eat-sleep-and-drink surf animal. However, as he grew older the peripatetic Horan became an unconventional and at times controversial figure, embracing unorthodox views on things such as lifestyle and surfboard design. He has strong opinions on issues such as pollution control and world peace.

Horan is a tough, uncompromising competitor with plenty of determination. Saddled when he was young with a reputation of being inadequate in big waves, Horan worked hard on that part of his surfing to develop into one of the sport's more daring and accomplished big-wave riders. A high point of the enigmatic Horan's career came in December 1989 when he easily won the Billabong Pro at Sunset Beach to join an elite few who have won contests in Hawaii and to accomplish the even rarer feat of winning back a place in the top 16 rankings.

Of their well publicised rivalry, Mark Richards says: 'Cheyne was pretty much my main rival in the years when I was trying to win the world title. There were a lot of guys who were hard to beat as well but Cheyne was the main one and I think everyone credits me with ruining Cheyne's life by the fact that he did not win a world title. But what they forget is that I only beat him three times and that it was Rabbit [Bartholomew] who beat him the other time. We have never been enemies but we have never been the best of friends either. We always said "Hello" and talked to each other but it is really hard to be friendly with someone you are competing against all the time, someone who could be standing in your way of winning a world title. It is an interesting relationship you have with them. You kind of wish a lot of the time they did not exist.

'But the fact that he came so close never came up for discussion between us. He has never said anything to me and I've never said anything to him about it but, strangely enough, I do not feel guilty about it but I do think about it at times. It made me stop and think in 1982 when I thought he might have won. I have often wondered how I would have coped if it had been me coming second. It would have been so hard to live with and deal with had the shoe been on the other foot. I feel for him.

'There was probably no-one more stoked for him than I was when he won the Billabong. It was the biggest and most desirable event to win at that stage and the $US50 000 first prize made me so happy for him. I had an ear to ear grin when I found out.'

A nimble surfer with a low centre of gravity and the light-footed agility to skip over the top of small, slow waves, Horan seldom conformed to general opinion when it came to surfboard design. In 1983 Horan shunned the increasingly-popular, three-fin boards, electing instead to fit the winged keel the late Ben Lexcen had designed for the 1983 America's Cup 12-metre yacht challenge. Winged keels on surfboards did not become popular whereas Simon Anderson's three-fin idea became universal. As Mark comments: 'Cheyne was a phenomenal, terrific surfer. I

Richards's classic bottom turn: it's easy after you've done thousands. This one is at Merewether Beach, Australia, in 1985. PHOTO: SURFING WORLD

Richards surfs Pinballs at Waimea Bay, Hawaii, in 1985.
PHOTO: BERNIE BAKER-LEONARD BRADY/ISLAND STYLE

Mark's backhand surfing was always strong, as he demonstrates in Hawaii.
PHOTO: BERNIE BAKER-LEONARD BRADY/ISLAND STYLE

Cheyne Horan gets radical on conventional equipment. The Richards/Horan rivalry was the greatest battle in pro surfing during the early 1980s. PHOTO: MARTIN TULLEMANS

time. While many haoles (non-Hawaiians) were steering clear of people like Eddie during these troubled times he was inviting Mark down to Waimea for lunch, when he would regale the wide-eyed youngster with chilling tales of riding giant surf. Mark was awestruck by the great man. Eddie Aikau drowned in March 1978. Aikau had been honoured with an invitation to join 15 others in a ceremonial and historic paddling journey from Hawaii to Tahiti in the canoe Holkule'a. Not long out of Honolulu huge seas capsized the boat and Eddie, because of his knowledge, strength and fitness, was given permission to try a 20km paddle to the island of Lanai to get help. He was never seen again. The other crew members were rescued unharmed.

Mark considers the attitude of the Hawaiians to the influx of Australian surfers: 'Considering how aggressive and how competitive we were in Hawaii in the 1970s and how successful we were in their contests I think the Hawaiians were pretty accommodating. The Australians were surfing big waves as though they were small waves, that is why we did so well. Some Australians started boasting in magazines, the Hawaiians became a bit incensed and offended. They did not really mind they had been beaten in the events but I think they got pissed off when they saw we were abusing their hospitality and gloating about our success. Rabbit wrote an article called "Bustin' Down The Door" and that really kicked it along. That was the beginning of it all, the start of the animosity and it's festered ever since. And what's helped to keep it alive is the growth of pro surfing. There have been more contests, more publicity, more prize money and so more and more people go to Hawaii each year and there's only so much the place can take. When I first went there in the early 70s there were no more than 15 Australians on the north shore for the winter. Now it's grown to anywhere up to 100

Australians, probably twice that number of Brazilians plus all the Japanese and the huge number of mainland Americans. It has to cause friction and animosity. If I lived in Hawaii and I went for six months without surf and all of a sudden the good surf season arrived and I had 100 Australians, 200 Brazilians, 50 Japanese and 300 Californians on my doorstep I would be a pretty mean person too. I would want my fair share. And I think you have a bit of racial tension thrown in as well, a black vs white thing. It's a problem and it's not going to end because the magazines drum into people that Hawaii is it, Hawaii is the place where you make or break your reputation. They gave Damien Hardman a hard time the first time he won the world title because at that stage he didn't have much of a big-wave reputation. The surfing media is virtually forcing people to go there and sacrifice themselves to the biggest, meanest wave that comes along to give them credibility. For people who keep returning to Hawaii my advice is that you should enjoy it as much as you can because the thing to keep in mind is that it is a little more crowded than it was last year but it's a lot less crowded than it will be next year. Having said all that, I think for the professional tour to remain viable Hawaii must be a part of it.'

Mark believes that even the Newcastle surfing scene is reaching saturation point. 'There are very few times when you can come out of the water and say you had a really great time. You can sit out the back and mind your own business, waiting for one good one, and when you go to take off some idiot who's been paddling all over the place and has already have five waves to your none paddles inside you and yells you off the wave. I come out of the water these days feeling more aggressive than relaxed. If you go into the surf in a relaxed, let's-have-a-good-time mode you will get taken advantage of. No-one gives you a fair turn. I have seen surfing develop almost from day one and the worst change is the whole localism thing that seems so prevalent in surfing these days. People on boards hate people on boogie boards and all this other stuff. It does not really matter. The ocean is there for people's enjoyment and if you want to ride waves on a piece of sponge or a glass fibre surfboard it doesn't matter. The whole gist of the thing is to go out and feel the pleasure of riding a wave. Then when you get Martin Potter, a former world champion, saying [in a 1991 magazine poll] that it was OK to run over boogie board riders it does not really help. I do not know if these modern professionals realise they have a great influence over what young kids think. If kids read what Martin said, and he obviously said it in jest, then some will start doing just that and people will get hurt. Professional surfers have a tremendous amount of responsibility because they are in the limelight. OK, so you think you are a bit of a renegade and you don't care about that stuff but you do have a responsibility because you put yourself in that situation. You are making a living out of the sport and you are a very fortunate person because you are making a living out of something you enjoy doing.'

Mark Richards, married to a lovely, vibrant woman, with two beautiful children, a dream home overlooking his favourite beach and a flourishing business, appeared to have reaped all the rewards of the modern achiever. He was, after all, living in paradise as the survey of Newcastle residents had discovered. Work is a few minutes easy drive away, Merewether's waves are a stroll down the beach and his neighbourhood is thick with lifelong friends. He could settle back among his trophies and his memorabilia and reflect he was the greatest, perhaps of all time, and maybe even more remarkably he didn't have an enemy to show for it. When

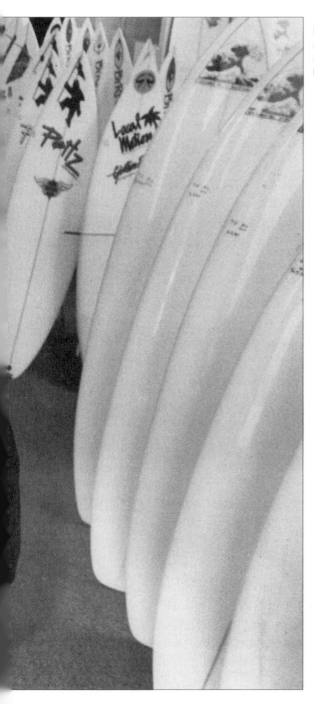

Life after competition surfing: Mark in his surf shop in Newcastle.
PHOTO: NEWS LIMITED

he's not 'playing with the tribe' he can strum his guitar, listen to his music (Bruce Springsteen's the great favourite) or read novels by authors such as Wilbur Smith, Nelson De Mille and Robert Ludlum. Nobody could suggest that Mark Richards isn't by and large a happy, contented, well adjusted and overwhelmingly grateful man. But things gnaw. First there is the back. It restricts his time in the water hugely just when, without the constraints of having something to prove, his surfing could be at its most expressive. Though he has more freedom than most to surf where and when he chooses he still has work and family, so surfing generally is restricted to Merewether. And while he loves his home break it still niggles that just getting a wave there can be such a source of friction.

From the beginning surfing to Mark was all about fun, not argument and hostility. Like many, but certainly not all, of the great Australian professional surfers Mark Richards is a genial, generous surfing companion. He revels in his own performance but also loves to see those around him deriving similar enjoyment from the ocean. It's understandable that Mark Richards, who never meant anyone any harm, feels aggrieved when far lesser surfers show such little respect.

But dealing with a painful back and overcrowded surf aren't his main challenges. He has family and he has work but when you have been the very best in the world at something and you are still in your thirties, the rest of your life can seem like a long time. 'The surf shop is an enjoyable business because you are dealing with things you are really interested in and you know about. Plus you are talking to people who are on the same wave length, talking to surfers with whom you have a common bond because you derive enjoyment from exactly the same thing. But the problem is that after life on the tour everything else can seem like an anti-climax. You have achieved something and you have done the most exciting thing possible to do. It is unbelievable, wandering around the world all year and getting paid to do it and spending three months surfing the biggest and best waves in the world, in Hawaii. It is pretty hard to top. Regardless of what you do and the challenge and the enjoyment you get from it, nothing compares with winning and sometimes that is difficult to deal with. I have a problem dealing with it. You long for those days again, not so much for the competitive success but I think you long for the free and easy lifestyle, being answerable to no-one but yourself. Your life changes and as much as I enjoy things now I do really miss the tour. It is very hard to just stop and settle into a normal lifestyle. It's such a change, such a complete 360, to settle into the 9 to 5 working routine, family commitments, weekend surfs. It's completely opposite to what I used to do and it's very hard to come to terms with. I feel like I am at a crossroads. Two-thirds of me has come to grips with the fact it's all over but the other third is longing for the old days. I have started to live for everyone else whereas for 10 or 15 years I lived just for myself and did not care about anyone else. A pro surfer has probably one of the most selfish lifestyles imaginable. It is such a change when you stop and are married and have kids and other things become important in your life. You have responsibilities to them and their future.'

For all his eloquence Mark sometimes shoots from the hip and gives more measured thought later. Somewhere in the preceding monologue is perhaps one of his great contradictions. Although his more public achievements may be behind him, what he is doing now, maintaining a business and helping to raise a family, are simply life goals that other people embrace without having first been four times world surfing champion. Mark Richards is still achieving, still meeting challenges, it's just that now these are more private and more mundane. They are probably no less important. In recent years the Association of Surfing Professionals has contemplated launching a masters circuit as tennis and golf have done. Would that be a way for Mark to recapture some of the old glamour? 'I think it would be a terrific idea if they had it but I could not compete because of my back. Realistically, my days are over. I am quite happy about that, too. I'm probably contradicting myself here but I have no desire to put a coloured t-shirt on again. But I think even if my back was OK I would not want to compete on a Masters circuit. When you have competed at the very top, with the elite in your sport, you don't want to go back and be a sideshow to what is now the main event. You are not the real show.'

Mark Richards has been dealt intelligence and sensitivity not always found in all sports champions. He attributes his ability to succeed beyond anybody's wildest dreams and at the same time never to lose life's real plot to the influence of his parents, his wife and his own normality. 'I'm normal', is a Mark Richards catchphrase. A random check in and out of the surfing world reveals universal admiration and liking for Mark Richards. Graham Cassidy is a man given to hyperbole yet his assessment of Mark Richards as Australia's greatest champion after Don Bradman bears scrutiny. How many Australian sports champions have been considered the greatest by so many for so long as Richards has? As a founder and driving force of professional surfing in Australia, Cassidy will forever be grateful to Richards for being such an exemplary champion just when the sport needed one most. While other surfers have been prolific winners none has championed, in the real sense, surfing as gallantly as Richards. Val Richards and Robbie Wood agree that Mark's image was largely inst-rumental in convincing BHP to sponsor Newcastle's professional contest from 1985 until 1990, after which the recession finally prevailed. Their point is that had Newcastle's great surfer been a person of a different character, a less personable, less diplomatic, less caring surfer than Mark Richards then one of the world tour's great events may never have happened. Significantly, people such as Tom Curren, Tom Carroll, Mark Occhilupo and Damien Hardman were Newcastle winners. They were the second wave of superstars, the beneficiaries of the Richards legacy. Bernie Baker has observed surfing and just about every other sport for 30 years. He has watched Richards develop from diffident teenager to consummate big-wave maestro. Baker is in no doubt that Mark Richards is one of the twentieth century's great sportspeople.

When Tom Carroll took over from Mark Richards as world champion, he was given his due at a lavish ceremony in Sydney. Carroll's succinct accolade that night was memorable. He said how proud he was to succeed 'this man' and gestured to the big, slightly stooped, smiling figure of Mark Richards who stood standing back from the spotlight and looked uncomfortable in his dinner suit. The people stood as one and cheered and cheered.

MILESTONES

1968   1st Newcastle cadets
1st Newcastle under 14 schoolboys
1st Merewether Surfboard Club cadets

1969   1st Newcastle cadets
1st Newcastle under 14 schoolboys
schoolboys
1st Merewether Surfboard Club cadets

1970   1st Newcastle juniors
1st Merewether Surfboard Club juniors

1972   1st Merewether Surfboard Club juniors
Member, Australian team, world titles, |
San Diego

1973   1st Australian juniors, Margaret River,
Western Australia
1st NSW juniors, Sydney
1st Newcastle juniors
1st Merewether Surfboard Club juniors

1974   1st Bells Beach eliminations
1st Mattara Open, Merewether,
Newcastle

1975 1st Bells Beach eliminations
1st Smirnoff Pro, Waimea Bay, Hawaii

1976 1st Men's Cup, Sunset Beach, Hawaii
1st 2SM/Coca Cola Surfabout, Sydney
3rd IPS world rankings

1977 5th International Professional Surfing
world rankings

1978 1st Rip Curl/Coca Cola Classic, Bells Beach,
Victoria
10th International Professional Surfing
world rankings

1979 1st International Professional Surfing
world rankings
1st Stubbies Classic, Burleigh Heads, Queensland
1st Rip Curl Classic, Bells Beach, Victoria
1st Niijima Pro, Japan
1st Hang Ten World Cup, Haleiwa, Hawaii
1st Duke Kahanamoku Classic, Sunset
Beach, Hawaii

1980 1st International Professional Surfing world
rankings
1st Rip Curl/Big M Classic, Bells Beach, Victoria
1st Gunston 500, Durban, South Africa
1st Hang Ten International, Durban, South Africa
1st Offshore Pipeline Masters, Pipeline, Hawaii

1981 1st International Professional Surfing world
rankings

1st Stubbies Classic, Burleigh Heads, Qld
1st Mainstay Magnum, Durban, South Africa
1st Instinct US Pro, Malibu, California

1982 1st International Professional Surfing world
rankings
1st Rip Curl/Brian Rochford Classic, Bells
Beach, Victoria
1st Gunston 500, Durban, South Africa

1983 24th Association of Surfing Professionals
world rankings

1984 20th Association of Surfing Professionals
world rankings

1985 23rd Association of Surfing Professionals
world rankings
1st Billabong Pro, Sunset Beach, Hawaii

1986 26th Association of Surfing Professionals
world rankings
1st Billabong Pro, Waimea Bay and Sunset
Beach, Hawaii

1987 54th Association of Surfing Professionals
world rankings
Anchorman, Merewether, 1987 Quiksilver
Surf League national teams titles

Professional victories before world tour	**3**
Professional victories on world tour	**17**
Non-rated professional victories	**1**

Total professional victories	**21**
Top 16 finishes	**7**
World titles	**4**

Anchorman, Merewether Surfboard Club, winner, 1987 Quiksilver Surf League national teams championship

Surfer magazine poll winner 1979, 1980, 1981, 1982

Surfing magazine Surfer Of The Year 1979, 1980, 1982

Sun/Caltex NSW Sportsman of the Year 1981. Finalist 1980, 1982

ABC Sportsman Of The Year finalist 1982, 1983

NSW Department of Sport and Recreation Hall Of Champions, inducted 1981

NBN Channel 3 Newcastle Sportsman of The Year 1979, 1980, 1981; special award for excellence 1982

Confederation of Australian Sport, Sport Australia awards, male athlete of the year, finalist 1981, 1983; best single sporting performance, finalist 1981, 1983

Association of Surfing Professionals services to the sport award, 1986

Australian Surfriders Association Hall Of Fame, inducted 1985

Newcastle Sporting Hall of Fame, inducted 1992

INDEX

Page numbers in italics refer to illustrations.